PLANNING CHART

Reproduce and use when planning your centers.

	GROUP TIME	CENTERS					
		Reading	Writing	Math	Science	Art	Dramatic Play
MON							
TUES							
WED							
THUR							
FRI							

Simple Centers
for Kindergarten

By
Kathleen M. Douglas

Cover Illustration by
Ann Lutnicki

Inside Illustrations by
Deborah A. Kirkeeide

Publisher
Instructional Fair • TS Denison
Grand Rapids, Michigan 49544

• •

CREDITS
Author: Kathleen M. Douglas
Cover Illustration: Ann Lutnicki
Inside Illustrations: Deborah A. Kirkeeide
Project Director/Editor:
    Debra Olson Pressnall
Cover Art Production: Darcy Bell-Myers
Graphic Layout: Deborah Hanson McNiff

ABOUT THE AUTHOR
Kathleen M. Douglas has fifteen years of teaching experience in early childhood education. She holds a B.S. in Elementary Education and an M.S. in Early Childhood Education. Kathy is presently the Associate Director at Florida State University's Alumni Village Child Development Center. She enjoys teaching young children as well as student teachers at the university. Kathy also devotes her time teaching other professionals in the field of early childhood education and presenting at local and national early childhood conferences.

Standard Book Number 1-56822-305-6
Simple Centers for Kindergarten
Copyright © 1997 by Instructional Fair • TS Denison
2400 Turner Avenue NW
Grand Rapids, Michigan 49544

Printed in the USA

HOW TO USE THE BOOK

The purpose of this book is to provide teachers with the means to create motivational learning centers that enhance a kindergarten curriculum through the use of thematic and independent activities. Each center is designed to review or enhance developmentally appropriate skills. By visiting the success-oriented centers independently, your young learners become better risk takers and grow in self-esteem.

Simple Centers for Kindergarten offers 25 center activities plus ideas for the dramatic play area for each theme. With these center activity ideas for 10 themes, you can set up centers that include:
- language arts activities that strengthen letter recognition skills, build phonemic awareness and encourage verbal and written expression,
- math activities that strengthen counting, shape identification, patterning, and measurement skills, examine number relationships and foster inquiry and problem solving,
- science activities that cater to children's natural curiosity about the world around them, and
- activities that encourage creative expression through art and dramatic play.

Young children are action-oriented learners who need plenty of opportunities to play, reflect on their work and interact with other children. It is the opinion of this author that the children should be actively engaged in learning. This is possible when children are given opportunities to practice new skills, learn new concepts, work independently, think creatively, and deal with thought-provoking questions. The 10 thematic units of study that are offered in *Simple Centers for Kindergarten* certainly should be of interest to your students. During the school year the children can learn about bears, bees, birds, colors, environmental issues, forest life, plants, and more.

As you plan your classroom environment for a specific theme, perhaps transforming it into a wilderness environment for the bears theme or a post office for the alphabet theme, gather related materials that you already have available for simple center activities, such as puzzles, flannel board aids, math manipulatives, picture books, and so on. Add to these materials by preparing the activities offered in this resource. To ensure that your prepared center materials are durable, you may wish to cover them with laminating materials or clear adhesive plastic. Finally, before storing the materials for each center activity, be sure to label the container and the area on the shelf with identical labels. This management tool is an effective measure for encouraging children to keep the center materials organized.

TABLE OF CONTENTS

ALL KINDS OF BEARS

Brown bears, black bears, sun bears, sloth bears, polar bears, spectacled bears! So much to learn about these fascinating mammals. Think about the polar bear, the king of the Arctic, as the animal walks across the large ice sheets of the polar region, hunting for seals, fish or walruses. Actually the polar bear is also a very good swimmer and fast sprinter. Its thick fur coat and padded feet keep the animal warm during very cold days. Now think about the giant brown bear, the king of the Alaskan wilderness, as this animal hunts for salmon during the spring season, or feasts on mice, ground squirrels, berries, and other plants. Not all bears are fast runners. The sloth bear, also called the honey bear, moves slowly through the grass and shrubs, searching for its favorite meal—honey. The sun bear is different from its relatives because it likes to hunt at night and nap in the trees during the day; in fact, it enjoys sunbathing while it sleeps. What do all bears have in common? How are they different? Where do they live? These are some questions children can think about as they study bears. Keep in mind that teddy bears can also have a part in this theme as you encourage the children to participate in imaginative activities.

Change your classroom into a wilderness environment by using the bear patterns on pages 12–14. Using the opaque projector, trace the bears on bulletin board paper and then paint them. Perhaps you might like to add scenery pieces to enhance your wilderness scene.

As you set up your centers, be sure to include books about bears and teddy bears for the children to read in your library corner. During group time talk about bears or read aloud informative picture books. The following books have useful information:
- Barrett, N. S. *Bears*. Franklin Watts, 1988.
- Betz, Dieter. *The Bear Family*. Tambourine Books, 1991.

· · · · · The Dramatic Play Center · · · · ·

Transform this area into a wilderness environment. If possible, set up an actual tent that does not need to be staked to the ground or hang a sheet as a tent. Roll newspapers into logs for the campfire. Also provide a picnic basket with play food, flashlights, star guides, nature guides, sleeping bags, and a backpack filled with some cooking gear. Make bear tracks to lead the child into a pretend forest area. Be imaginative! The center can be a wonderful play area for creative young minds.

ACTIVITIES FOR CURRICULUM AREAS

READING & LANGUAGE DEVELOPMENT CENTER ACTIVITIES

· · · · · My Bear Story · · · · ·

Materials Needed: pattern on page 11, construction paper, markers, scissors, tape recorder, blank cassette tapes

Directions: Why did the bear climb the tree? Is danger near? Children will delight in telling a story about the bear family. To set up the center, reproduce the pattern page and mount it on construction paper. Cut apart the cards and color them if desired. Invite the child to study the cards carefully and tell her partner a story about the pictures. Perhaps the child may enjoy recording her story on cassette tape and then listening to it later.

Variation: Set the stage for "big" stories. Enlarge the pictures on 11" x 17" (279 x 432 mm) copier paper and display them in the language arts center. Another idea for storytelling is to encourage the children to create their own stories. Using craft sticks and construction paper, let the children make stick puppets for their stories. During group time the "storytellers" may need help telling their stories by inviting volunteers from the audience to hold the stick puppets or to dramatize the events of the stories.

· · · · · Talking About Bears · · · · ·

Materials Needed: patterns on pages 12 and 14, felt fabric (various colors for bears and scenery), scissors, flannel board, fabric marker

Directions: Enlarge the patterns before cutting them out of felt. Using a fabric marker, draw distinguishing details on the felt shapes. Place the shapes on a flannel board or in a small basket. Encourage the children to talk about bears as they place the felt pieces on the flannel board.

Variation: Supply additional copies of the pattern pieces, craft sticks, markers or crayons, and scissors for stick puppets. Transform a few large-size shoe boxes into a stage, and your future playwrights are set to produce one-act plays.

• • • • • "Beary" Cool Words • • • • •

Materials Needed: patterns on page 13, construction paper or poster board, markers, scissors, glue

Directions: Children can match words or letters written on furry bears. To prepare the materials, reproduce the bears on the pattern page, making enough copies for the words or letters you would like the children to match. Mount the bears on construction paper and cut out. Color the Kodiak bears if desired. Using a marker write the word or letter on two bears to make a matching pair. Continue until you have the desired number of bears. In the center, invite eager learners to find all of the matching pairs.

• • • • • Bear Lotto • • • • •

Materials Needed: patterns on page 15 and 16, construction paper, markers, scissors, glue

Directions: This visual discrimination activity can easily be adapted to meet the needs of your young learners. Decide if the children will match pictures or words. If the children are matching pictures, make two copies of page 15. If the children are matching pictures with words, photocopy pages 15 and 16. Mount the copies on construction paper. Cut apart one set of the picture cards to make the playing cards. In the center, invite the child to match the picture cards with pictures or words on the playing board.

• • • • • Teddy Bear Rhymes • • • • •

Materials Needed: pattern on page 17, construction paper, markers, scissors, glue

Directions: Touch your toes. Find your nose. Think about Teddy Bear's actions and match the rhyming words. For this activity, introduce the traditional rhyme, "Teddy Bear, Teddy Bear, Turn Around" during group time. Talk about the rhyming words that are heard at the end of the lines. To prepare the center materials, reproduce the pattern page and mount it on the construction paper. Cut apart the cards and color them as desired. Now the materials are ready for the child to identify the matching pairs by placing them together on a tabletop.

Variation: Invite the child to "read" the cards to a partner who acts out what Teddy Bear is doing.

13

 # Bear Lotto

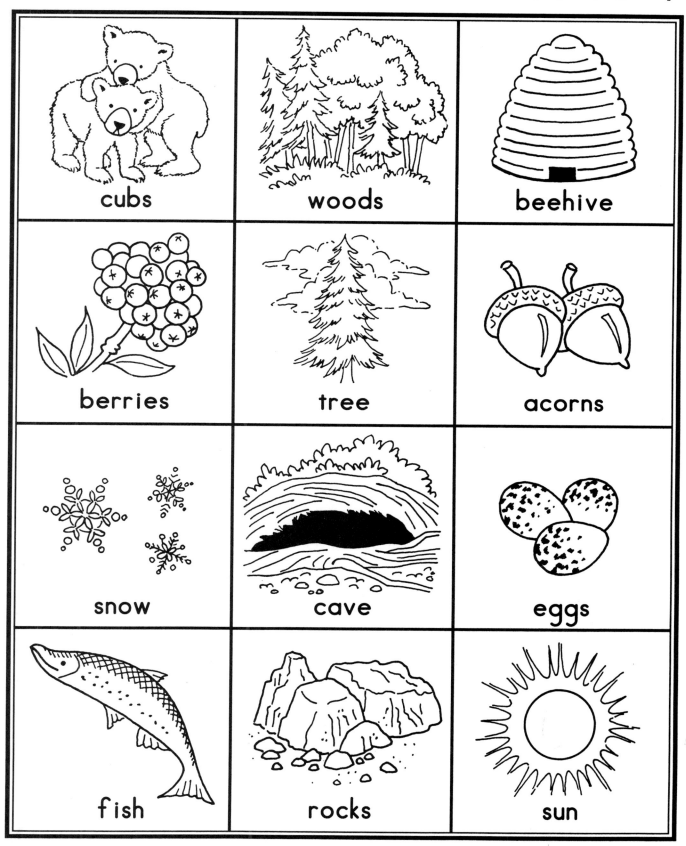

cubs	woods	beehive
berries	tree	acorns
snow	cave	eggs
fish	rocks	sun

# Bear Lotto

cubs	woods	beehive
berries	tree	acorns
snow	cave	eggs
fish	rocks	sun

Teddy Bear, turn around.

Teddy Bear, touch the ground.

Teddy Bear, touch your head.

Teddy Bear, make your bed.

Teddy Bear, find your nose.

Teddy Bear, touch your toes.

WRITING CENTER ACTIVITIES

· · · · · All About Bears · · · · ·

Materials Needed: patterns on pages 13–15, construction paper, newsprint, stapler or yarn and hole punch, scissors, paste, pencils, markers

Directions: Here is an idea for making booklets to help children share what they have learned about bears. The child can choose which bear to feature on the booklet cover, such as the polar bear, Kodiak bear or one of the other bears shown on page 14. Assemble a few sheets of newsprint for the booklet pages and cover with construction paper. Staple or tie the pages together with yarn. Provide reproduced copies of the pattern for the child to use when writing about bears. Some children may wish to use the small pictures to write rebus stories.

Variation: Decorate the learning center with pictures and words. Just enlarge the small lotto board pictures (page 15) and display them on poster board. If appropriate, young writers can copy the words on bear shape word cards.

· · · · · "Beary" Fine Printing · · · · ·

Materials Needed: fresh or frozen berries, plastic container with lid, craft sticks, newsprint or bear shapes (pattern page 13), vinegar, smock

Directions: Crush the berries and strain the seeds from the juice. Add a very small amount of vinegar to the juice. Using craft sticks, the children can draw the letter "Bb" or print short words with the berry juice on blank paper or bear shapes. (You may wish to have the child wear a smock while printing to prevent permanent juice stains on clothing.)

Variation: If children have teddy bears, they can print the first letters of the bears' names on copies of the pattern on page 20. Each child can use this page as part of the booklet "Me and My Teddy Bear." The book *Alphabear* by Kathleen Hague (Henry Holt & Company, 1984) is perfect for introducing names of teddy bears. When the children are finished with their "berry" fine prints, share the prints during group time and talk about which letters of the alphabet are shown.

· · · · · Me and My Teddy Bear · · · · ·

Materials Needed: teddy bears from home, construction paper, newsprint, crayons, pencils, stapler or yarn and hole punch, pattern on page 20, *The Teddy Bears' Picnic* by Jimmy Kennedy (Bedrick/Blackie, 1987)

Directions: We can write teddy bear adventures. Perhaps you would like to host a teddy bear day and invite children to bring their bears to school. Be sure to provide some "adopted bears" for children who do not have them at home. During group time share some picture books about teddy bears and their adventures, such as *The Teddy Bears' Picnic* by Jimmy Kennedy. In the writing center, provide copies of the booklet cover mounted on construction paper along with paper for writing the stories. Encourage the child to write an adventure story for his teddy bear. When finished, assemble the pages along with the cover to make the booklet. Staple or tie yarn to bind the booklet.

· · · · · Lacing Bears · · · · ·

Materials Needed: shoelace or yarn, masking tape, poster board, patterns on pages 13 and 23, scissors, glue, markers, hole punch

Directions: Young fingers will delight in lacing these cute bears. Reproduce the large teddy bear. Enlarge and reproduce the polar and Kodiak bears. Mount the copies on poster board. Cut out the bears and color them as desired. Punch holes along the outer edges of the cutouts and along the stitching on the teddy bear. Cut pieces of yarn 18" (457 mm) in length. Wrap masking tape around one end of each string. Tie the other end of the string to the bear shape. Your bears are ready for lacing.

· · · · · Honey Bear Prints · · · · ·

Materials Needed: shaving cream, yellow food coloring, large trays or tabletop, bowl, spray bottle, water, smock

Directions: Fill a bowl with shaving cream and gently mix yellow food coloring in it. In the center the children can print "Bb" in the honey-colored cream on trays or the tabletop. Just smoothen the cream to make the letters disappear. Spray a small amount of water on the shaving cream if it starts to dry. This activity will be a favorite.

Variations: Provide a copy of the "Bear Lotto" cards for the children to use when printing words in the shaving cream.

All About My Teddy Bear

MATH CENTER ACTIVITIES

· · · · · Big to Little Bears · · · · ·

Materials Needed: patterns on page 13, construction paper, scissors, glue, markers

Directions: Arranging bears from smallest to largest or vice versa can be a challenging task if the bears are close in size. Reproduce the polar and Kodiak bears by photocopying the images at the following percentages: 60%, 80%, 100%, 120%, and 140%. Mount the bears on construction paper and cut out the shapes. Have the children arrange the bears by size.

· · · · · Counting Crunchy, Munchy Acorns · · · · ·

Materials Needed: patterns on page 23, poster board, markers, 75 acorns or acorn caps, 10 spring clothespins, clean plastic frosting container with lid, red checkered piece of cloth

Directions: Bears just love crunchy, munchy acorns. Hopefully young learners will love to feed these teddy bears their favorite snack. To prepare the materials for this activity, reproduce six copies of the teddy bear. Mount them on poster board and cut out the shapes. Color as desired. Write a different number on each clothespin (1–10 or 6–15) and glue an acorn shape on each one for decoration. Place the clothespins in the plastic container. In the center encourage the child to draw six clothespins and fasten each one on a teddy bear's arm. Let the child feed each bear the corresponding number of acorns because it is a picnic. Be sure to use the checkered table-cloth.

Variation: For children having strong math skills, provide dice along with two teddy bears and 40 acorns. The children can take turns rolling a die and filling each bear's tummy with acorns. When 20 acorns have been placed on each bear the game ends.

· · · · · Bears 'n' Berries Patterning · · · · ·

Materials Needed: patterns on pages 23–24, construction paper, scissors, glue, markers

Directions: Bears love berries and so will your children with this delightful repeat patterning activity. Reproduce 20–30 copies of the picture cards (see page 23) for the children to use. Use a few cards to begin patterns on the patterning mat (see page 24). Tape the cards in place and make a photocopy of the patterning mat. Rearrange the cards for new patterns and make a second copy of the mat. Now the children will have four patterns to finish. Mount all of the copies on construction paper. Cut apart the pattern cards and color all of the materials as desired. Set the materials in a labeled container so the children can have a "berry" good time with patterns.

· · · · · "Beary" Good Counting · · · · ·

Materials Needed: pattern on page 23, milk jug caps, poster board, index cards, markers

Directions: How many faces will cover the honey pot? This and other questions will spur young minds to investigate how size makes a difference. On poster board draw two different-size honey pots. As you draw the honey pots, think about how many milk jug caps will be needed to cover them. Size the pots accordingly. Color them as desired and cut out the shapes. (Be sure to use a different color for each honey pot.) Collect milk jug caps that can also be used for the Earth-Friendly Care theme. Glue a bear face (see pattern page 22) on each milk jug cap. For this activity have the child cover each honey pot with milk jug caps and then gather the milk jug caps into two piles and compare the size of the piles. Ask the child to estimate: Which pile has fewer caps? Invite the child to count the caps and compare the quantities. (Provide a copy of the counting board on page 47 for the child to use when counting the caps.) Give the child two index cards which have simple drawings of each honey pot. Ask the child to record how many caps cover each honey pot.

Variation: Some children may need additional practice in sorting objects by color. To provide these opportunities make 30–40 bear faces and color them with different colors.

· · · · · How Tall Is the Bear? · · · · ·

Materials Needed: pattern on page 23, milk jug caps, construction paper, scissors, glue, markers

Directions: Check out the heights of the cute teddy bears by measuring them with milk jug caps. (If you prefer, use the milk jug caps from the previous activity.) To prepare the materials, photocopy the teddy bear pattern at 100% and 150%. Mount the copies on construction paper and cut out the shapes. Color the bears as desired. Encourage the child to measure the heights of the bears and compare the measurements.

Variation: Real bears vary in length from 3 ft or .9 m (sun bear) to 9 ft. or 2.7 m (Alaskan brown bear). If you would like to make giant room decorations, enlarge the bear patterns (see pages 13–14) to actual size on bulletin board paper with the opaque projector. The children will marvel at how large the bears actually are. If the bears are displayed on the wall near the floor, invite the children to use common objects to measure their lengths.

Counting Crunchy Munchy Acorns Patterns/
Bears 'n' Berries Patterns

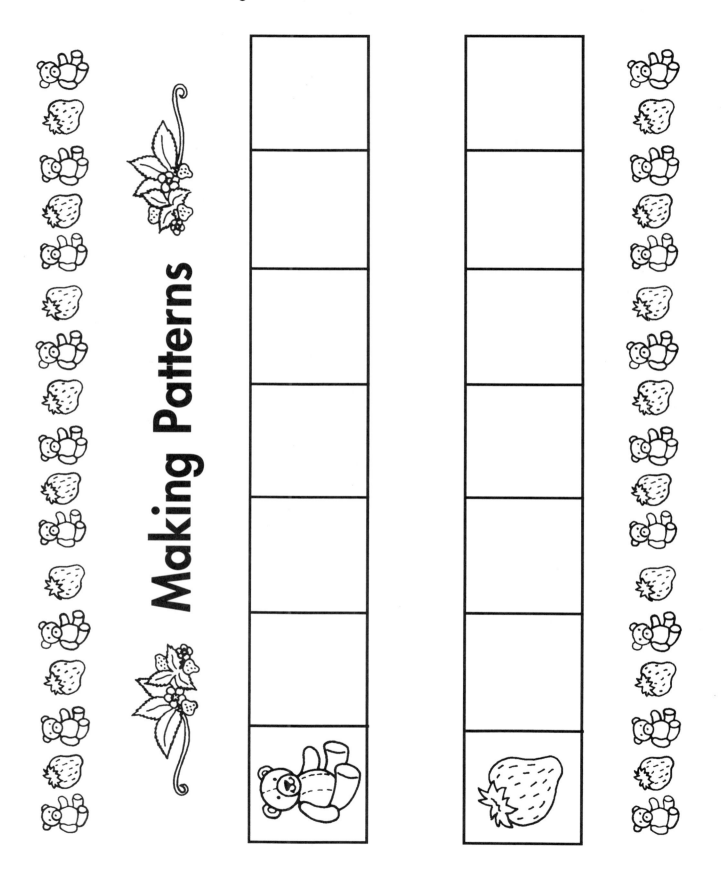

Making Patterns

SCIENCE CENTER ACTIVITIES

· · · · · Sticky and Wet Investigations · · · · ·

Materials Needed: small amount of honey in squeeze bottle, water in squeeze bottle, waxed paper, pencil, paper, magnifying glass, newspaper, pattern on page 27

Directions: What do you notice when you look at something with a magnifying glass? Explore the room and look for things that have fibers, things that are smooth or rough, and things that are composed of small particles. To prepare the materials, provide a copy of the upper left-hand picture card on page 27 along with magnifying glasses. Encourage the children to investigate how objects look when magnified. For another investigation, encourage the children to observe how drops of honey and water act as a magnifier. First, place a piece of waxed paper on the newspaper, and then have the child place drops of honey and water on the waxed paper and examine the newspaper through the drops.

Variation: Will pancake syrup drops act as a magnifier? Corn syrup drops? Perhaps the children may be interested in investigating other liquids that are sticky.

· · · · · "Beary" Good Snacks · · · · ·

Materials Needed: different food samples that have strong odors (freshly cut onion, garlic, sauerkraut) and foods that have light odors (strawberries, apples, blueberries, raspberries), small containers, file folder, patterns on page 27, scissors, glue

Directions: Bears depend on their sense of smell instead of sight when searching for food. Like the bears, the children can determine if each food has a light or strong odor. To prepare the materials, gather food samples and place them in small containers with lids. Punch a few holes in the lids to allow the odors to escape. Photocopy and cut out the pictures of the bears smelling foods. Glue each picture on one half of the folder. In the center, encourage the children to smell the foods and then place each container in the corresponding section of the folder. Let the children discuss the results of their observations. (There may be disagreements about which foods have unpleasant odors.) This is a perfect opportunity to graph the results as each child completes the activity.

· · · · · Shake and Listen · · · · ·

Materials Needed: objects to shake, plastic margarine containers with lids, permanent marker, pattern on page 27

Directions: Listen carefully for noises, just like bears who depend on their sense of hearing as well as smell for keeping safe. To prepare the materials, select several items that differ in sound when shaken. For example, small amounts of rice and dried beans can be selected for noise makers. Pour the same amount of each substance in two containers. (Be sure to number each container on the bottom and record the matching pairs on an answer key.) Use tape to secure the lids. Provide a copy of the upper right-hand picture card on page 27 along with the materials in a labeled container. Now the materials are ready. Have the child shake each container and match the containers that sound alike. When finished, compare the results with the answer key. For another investigation, let children make additional sets for others to match.

· · · · · Matching Cubs with Mothers · · · · ·

Materials Needed: pattern on page 28, construction paper, scissors, glue, markers

Directions: For this activity young learners must look for distinguishable details before matching mother bears with cubs. To prepare the picture cards, enlarge the pattern page by photocopying it on 11" x 17" (279 x 432 mm) paper. Mount the copy on construction paper and cut apart the pictures. Color them if desired. To make the pictures self-checking, code them with numbers or letters on the backs. Now this matching activity is ready for young learners.

· · · · · Bear Food Classification · · · · ·

Materials Needed: pattern on page 23 (a bear head), magazines, scissors, marker, construction paper, glue, file folder, pattern on page 27 (bear smelling onion, bear smelling berries)

Directions: What foods do bears eat? For this activity, clip pictures from magazines of food items, toys, household items, tools, etc. for children to sort. Glue these pictures on construction paper. Reproduce the bear head pattern as many times as necessary to correspond to the number of pictures of foods that bears like. Glue them on the backs of the corresponding pictures. Reproduce the picture cards on page 27. Glue the picture of the bear smelling an onion on one section of the file folder. Glue the picture of the bear near the berries on the other section. Store all of the materials in a large envelope. During group time discuss what bears eat and show pictures of these foods. Also discuss pictures of nonfood items. In the center, have the child sort the pictures accordingly and then check her work by turning the picture cards *face down* to find out which ones have bears heads on the backs.

ART CENTER ACTIVITIES

· · · · · Tissue Bears · · · · ·

Materials Needed: tissue paper (brown, black, white), markers, glue, paper, paintbrush

Directions: Cut the tissue paper into 3" (76 mm) squares. Place the gathered materials in a bin for storage. Add a very small amount of water to thin the glue. Have the children draw bears and then cover the bears with glue. Finish the bears by placing tissue paper in the glue. Help the child to notice the lighter and darker areas of color which occur because some pieces of paper overlap.

· · · · · Large Furry Bears · · · · ·

Materials Needed: cotton balls, paper toweling, cloth scraps, handled sponges, tempera paints, Styrofoam trays, newsprint, scissors

Directions: How can a bear be painted to look furry? Try painting with handled sponges, wads of paper, or cotton balls. To prepare the materials, cut large bear shapes from newsprint or encourage each child to draw a very large bear on the paper. Provide paint along with other materials for the child to use to paint a furry bear. Show the child how to dip the wad of paper toweling, handled sponge, cloth, or cotton balls in a small amount of tempera paint and then lightly pat the paper to make the paint look textured. Continue until the bear is covered with paint. Some children may use other colors of paint to make distinguishing marks on their bears.

· · · · · Yummy Cupcake Creations · · · · ·

Materials Needed: cake mix and baking utensils, frosting, sprinkles, round candies and other food items for cake decorating

Directions: These tasty cupcake treats can be prepared with the children. Prepare the cake batter by following the instructions on the box and then bake the cupcakes. Allow them to cool. At the appropriate time, have each child create a bear face on a cupcake with sprinkles, candies and frosting. Enjoy the snack.

· · · · · Painting with Brown · · · · ·

Materials Needed: tempera paint (red, blue, yellow), paintbrushes, paper, clean Styrofoam trays

Directions: Which paint colors can be mixed together to make brown? Here is the perfect opportunity for children to experiment with primary colors. Encourage the children to mix different colors together until brown is made. Have them use their brown paint to paint bears on large sheets of paper. Forest scenery can be added by mixing yellow and blue together to make green for trees.

Variation: Create bear prints for the children to paint. Locate a diagram of a bear's front and hind tracks in an encyclopedia or identification guide. From corrugated cardboard cut out pieces that resemble parts of the tracks and glue them on another piece of cardboard. When the model is finished, show the children how they can make prints by using a paintbrush to cover the model with paint. Then turn the model *face down* on paper and press to transfer the shape.

· · · · · Bear Sculptures · · · · ·

Materials: project clay, craft sticks, plastic forks, pictures of bears

Directions: With pictures of bears displayed in prominent places young artists can mold play clay into bear figurines. To provide the clay for this activity, follow the recipe shown below. You may wish to make the clay in a variety of natural fur colors as well as bright colors for scenery. Just store the clay in plastic storage containers or resealable plastic bags. When the children are finished sculpting bears, allow the bears to air dry while being displayed in the art center.

Project Clay
2 cups (474 ml) all-purpose flour
1 cup (237 ml) salt
½–1 cup (118–237 ml) water
2 Tbsp. (29.6 ml) vegetable oil

Combine the ingredients in a mixing bowl and knead until smooth. Place the finished projects on waxed paper or aluminum foil (if baking them). They will air dry in a few days or you may bake them at low heat.

ALPHABET ANTICS

So many delightful experiences involve print! Wonderful picture books that touch the heart, postcards from family members and friends, and birthday cards are just a few examples. Perhaps your young learners are becoming aware of letters and words on billboards, traffic signs, business signs, and license plates as well as in magazines and on cereal boxes. This unit offers a host of ideas to extend the children's interest in print. Using the opaque projector enlarge any of the patterns on the following pages on bulletin board paper and paint them for large wall decorations.

In addition to the center activities that are offered in this theme, gather other alphabet materials for instant centers: ABC lacing beads, wooden puzzles and floor puzzles, a letter jar, alphabet puppets, a magnetic alphabet board, and so on. As you set up the learning environment, provide a variety of alphabet books for the children to "read" in the library corner. The following books are wonderful to share during group time:

- Johnson, Stephen T. *Alphabet City.* Viking, 1995.
- Neumeier, Marty and Byron Glaser. *Action Alphabet.* Greenwillow, 1985.
- Rule, Michael J. *Erni Cabat's Magical ABC: Animals Around the Farm.* Harbinger House, 1992.
- Shannon, George. *Tomorrow's Alphabet.* Illus. by Donald Crews. Greenwillow Books, 1996.

· · · · · The Dramatic Play Center · · · · ·

Transform the center into a post office. Gather pencils, crayons, markers, stickers, envelopes, construction paper, paper, index cards, postal hats, mail bins, junk mail (donated by parents), rubber stamps and stamp pads, mail bags, small shoe boxes for mail boxes, stamp posters and other information from the U.S. postal service. Create four residential mailboxes by photocopying the house patterns on page 44 and cutting them apart. Glue each one on the end of a box. Print an address for each house. Set up the center with signs and other props and then open the doors for business. In the center the children can work in the post office, write letters to be mailed, deliver mail to the four residential mailboxes, and so on. Some of the mail for these houses could be addressed in the writing center.

ABCDEF

ACTIVITIES FOR CURRICULUM AREAS

ABCDEF

READING & LANGUAGE DEVELOPMENT CENTER ACTIVITIES

· · · · · Chitchat · · · · ·

Materials Needed: cassette recorder, microphone, blank tapes, alphabet books

Directions: What a delightful way to encourage children to "read" alphabet books and listen to their stories! Invite the child to speak into the microphone while reading the story. Replay the story for the child to hear.

Variation: Perhaps the child may prefer to work with a partner when recording the alphabet book. Have one child say the letter and the other answer by "reading" the name of the picture or text on the page.

· · · · · Letter Puzzles · · · · ·

Materials Needed: large-size letter stencils, crayons, scissors, poster board, construction paper, envelopes, marker

Directions: Here is an opportunity for the children to make their own alphabet puzzles. Using the opaque projector enlarge the stencils on poster board by tracing the letters. Cut out the new stencils and place them with crayons or pencils, scissors and construction paper in a labeled container. The children may make letter puzzles by selecting stencils and tracing them on construction paper, cutting out the letters and then cutting each letter into three to five pieces. Place each individual letter puzzle in an envelope. Now the puzzles are ready to be assembled. Invite the child to assemble her puzzle or another one.

Variation: Special alphabet puzzles can be made with children's pictures. To prepare for this delightful activity, gather individual pictures of the children in your classroom and make photocopies of the prints. Provide these copies along with copies of pattern page 35. A child can make his puzzle by gluing his picture on the lower half of the puzzle and printing the first letter of his name on the upper portion of the puzzle. When finished, cut apart the two portions with a zigzag or interlocking puzzle cut. Keep the puzzle pieces in a special container. When several puzzles have been made, the children must match the pictures with letters before assembling the puzzles.

····· Roll-A-Letter Match ·····

Materials Needed: large colorful poster board letters made from stencils or commercially-made letters (foam, plastic, wood), pattern on page 36, tagboard, scissors, math counters

Directions: Just roll a letter and find its large matching partner. To prepare the materials, make a copy of the pattern page, mount it on tagboard and then form the cube by cutting out the pattern and folding on the dashed lines. Tape where necessary to finish the cube. As you collect materials, decide which letters will be featured in this game and if the children will be matching capitals with lowercase letters (or vice versa) or the same case. Print one letter on each face of the cube or use the prepared pattern die. (Be sure to draw a red line near the bottom of each letter on the cube to help the child read the letter.) When finished, gather the same letters (capitals and/or lowercase) formed in plastic, foam, or printed on wood. Place the cube and two or three of each featured letter along with other letters in a labeled container. When the children are ready to play the game have them decide how many times each player may take a turn, keeping track by collecting math counters. Now the children are ready to start the game by rolling the cube and finding the matching letter. The game ends when the children have completed a specified number of rolls. Encourage the children to determine which letter was collected the most number of times or the least number of times.

····· Alphabet Antics Game ·····

Materials Needed: game board patterns on pages 37–39, poster board, markers, glue, milk jug caps, permanent marker

Directions: Take a close look at these delightful alphabet animals. Children can practice matching capitals with lowercase letters. Just collect 26 milk jug caps and print the lowercase letters on the caps with a permanent marker. Reproduce the game board patterns by enlarging the images before duplicating them on large copier paper. Mount the game board on poster board and color the pictures as desired. For the activity have the child match the lowercase letter with the capital letter by placing it on the board.

····· ABC in a Row ·····

Materials Needed: Alphabet Antics game board for reference, large stencil letters, wallpaper samples, scissors, tagboard

Directions: Use stencils to make large-size letters from textured wallpaper samples. Mount the letters on tagboard and cut them out. (Be sure to mark the bottom of letters which are easily confused.) Invite the child to work with a partner and place the letters in order on the floor along a wall. *Note:* Be sure to adapt the activity for those children who are only able to work with half of the alphabet.

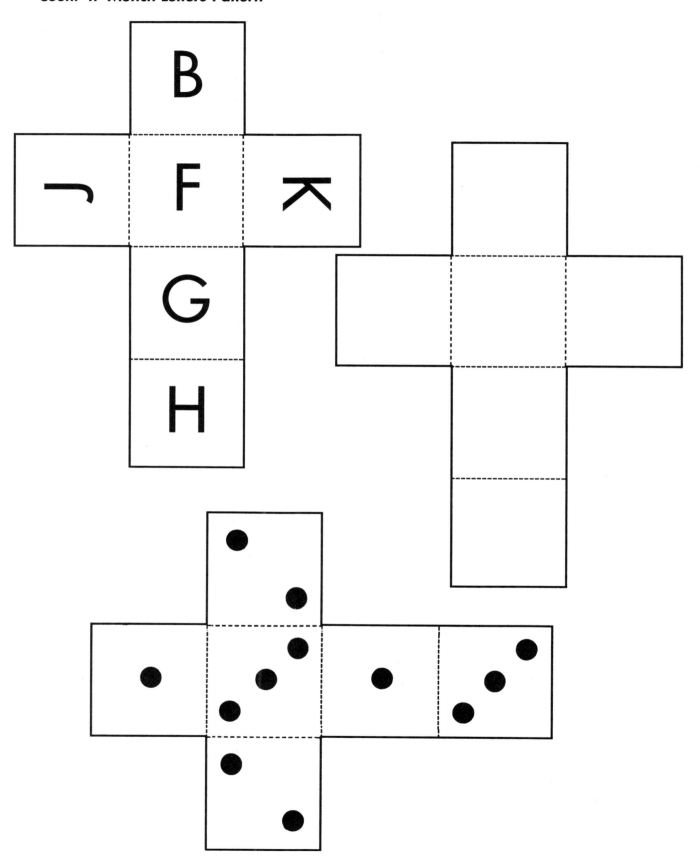

Glue here.

38

Glue here.

WRITING CENTER ACTIVITIES

· · · · · Alphabet Book Fun · · · · ·

Materials Needed: paper, colored pencils, stencils, stapler

Directions: Here is an opportunity for children to make booklets. To make a booklet have each child fold sheets of paper in half and staple them together along the left edge of the cover. (If several pages are made for the booklet, provide a hole punch and paper fasteners for the child to use.) Encourage the child to finish his booklet by drawing a cover design and printing letters, words and symbols in the booklet.

Variation: Some children may be interested in making their own ABC books. Encourage them to clip pictures and words from magazines to glue on booklet pages, print with rubber stamps (letters and/or pictures) and stamp pads, and draw pictures to complete the pages.

· · · · · Alphabet Peek and Guess · · · · ·

Materials Needed: small stencils, crayons, scissors, 3" x 4" (76 x 102 mm) construction paper pieces (cut a hole in each piece with a craft knife), magazines, catalogs, department store sales flyers, patterns on page 42–43, alphabet picture card set (optional)

Directions: This delightful book will surely entertain emergent readers as they look at the pages and peek under the flaps. To prepare for the activity, share Tana Hoban's book *Take Another Look* (Greenwillow, 1981) to help the children understand how to make the "Peek and Guess" book. In the center have each child create a page for the "Alphabet Peek and Guess" book. To do this, encourage the child to choose a letter and glue a corresponding picture on construction paper. If she is having difficulty in selecting a letter, encourage her to look at the picture cards for an idea. When the child is ready to finish the page, cut a hole in a piece of construction paper and then glue it to the page like a flap. *Note:* Before gluing the flap in place check to be sure a portion of the picture is visible through the hole in the flap. At the top of this flap page, print the following sentence: "It starts with _____." This sentence may be printed on sentence strips for the children to glue in place on the picture pages. Have each child complete the sentence by printing the first letter of the featured object's name. Assemble the book when all of the pages are finished and staple them together along the left edge of the cover. Now you are ready to take a peek at all of the interesting things the children chose for the booklet.

· · · · · Print 'n' Match · · · · ·

Materials Needed: variety of interesting objects (flowers, beads, toys, small plastic animals), index cards, pencils, paper

Directions: Using objects and word cards, the children will be busy printing letters or words for this activity. To set up the materials, gather five to six objects that have names that begin with specific consonants, such as ball and balloon for "Bb," toy dog for "Dd," and so on. Print the name (or initial consonant) of each selected object on an index card. Set the items on a tray and place the cards near the corresponding objects. Encourage the child to copy the names of the objects on paper. (If the child is making an ABC book, encourage her to write the words in her book.) When she is finished, have her remove the name cards from the objects, mix the order of the cards, and then match them with the corresponding objects.

Variation: Have the children address "envelopes" for the post office by copying the addresses that are used for the houses on pattern page 44.

· · · · · My "Newspaper" · · · · ·

Materials Needed: glue sticks, newspaper articles that have large letters and colorful print, paper, pencils

Directions: Some children may enjoy making their own "newspapers." Encourage them to create their newspapers by clipping letters, words, sentences, and pictures from newspaper articles and pasting them on construction paper or newsprint.

Variation: Invite the child to search for certain letters in a section of the newspaper and circle them with a highlighter marker. Have him count the circled letters. Which letter is circled the most often? the least often?

· · · · · Postcards · · · · ·

Materials Needed: glue sticks or paste, index cards, markers, newspaper pictures, pencils, comics strips, advertisements

Directions: Children can make "postcards" to send to family members by gluing pictures on index cards and then printing a message on the back of each card. Just gather various pictures from newspapers and magazines for them to use.

Peek and Guess

Walk with me and take a peek

At all the things that we can seek!

Look closely and see . . .

What do you think it could be?

· · · · · Sizing Up Silly Letters · · · · ·

Materials Needed: pattern on page 48, construction paper, scissors, glue

Directions: Enlarge and photocopy the pattern on large copier paper and mount it on construction paper. Cut apart the letters. Have the child arrange the letters by height—shortest to tallest or vice versa.

· · · · · Big "B" Measurement · · · · ·

Materials Needed: tagboard or bulletin board paper, capital "I" in foam, plastic or wood, craft materials

Directions: For this activity "Big B" needs to be measured. How tall is "Big B"? Is it taller or shorter than _____ (child's name)? To prepare the materials for this investigation, draw a giant size "B" on tagboard or bulletin board paper. Decorate "Big B" with craft materials to give the letter a personality. Now the activity materials are ready. Using several foam, plastic or wood capital "I"s have the children measure the height of "Big B." Encourage the children to compare their measurements and record them on paper. (If the foam and plastic letters differ in height, the children's measurements will vary.) Be sure to let the children talk about their results.

· · · · · Count 'n' Munch Letters · · · · ·

Materials Needed: alphabet cereal pieces, small scoop, paper towels, cube pattern on page 36, tagboard

Directions: Here is the scoop for this math game. To prepare the materials, provide alphabet cereal pieces along with the die on the pattern page. Make a copy of the pattern and mount it on tagboard. Cut out the die pattern. Fold on the dashed lines to form a cube. Tape the edges to secure them in place. In the center, have the children work with partners. Pour a small amount of cereal on a paper towel and also give each player two paper towel sections. Begin the game by having each child roll the die and collect the corresponding number of cereal pieces. These pieces are set on the waxed paper. When a player has collected 10 cereal pieces, the pieces are set aside as a set and play continues. When both players have collected 20 pieces each the game ends. It is snack time!

My Counting Board

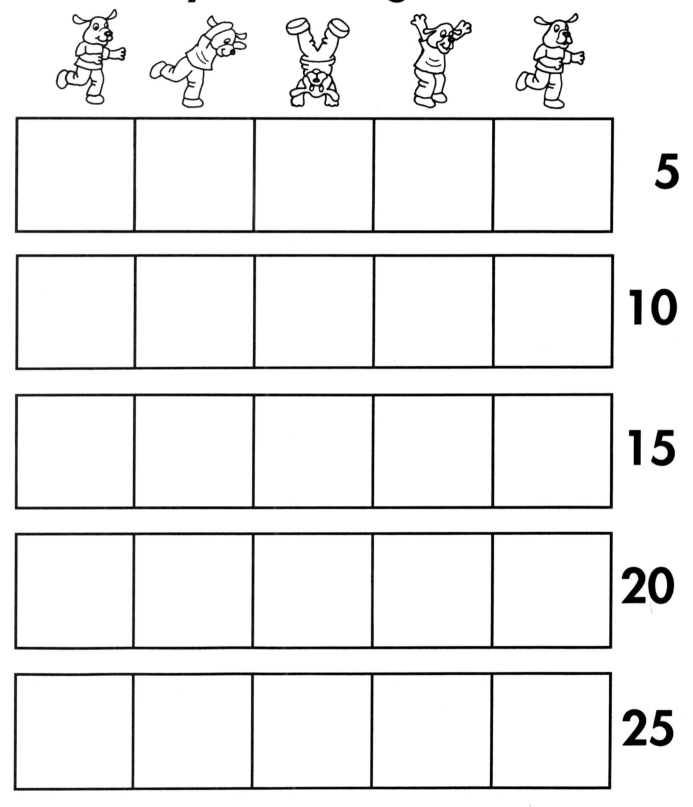

5

10

15

20

25

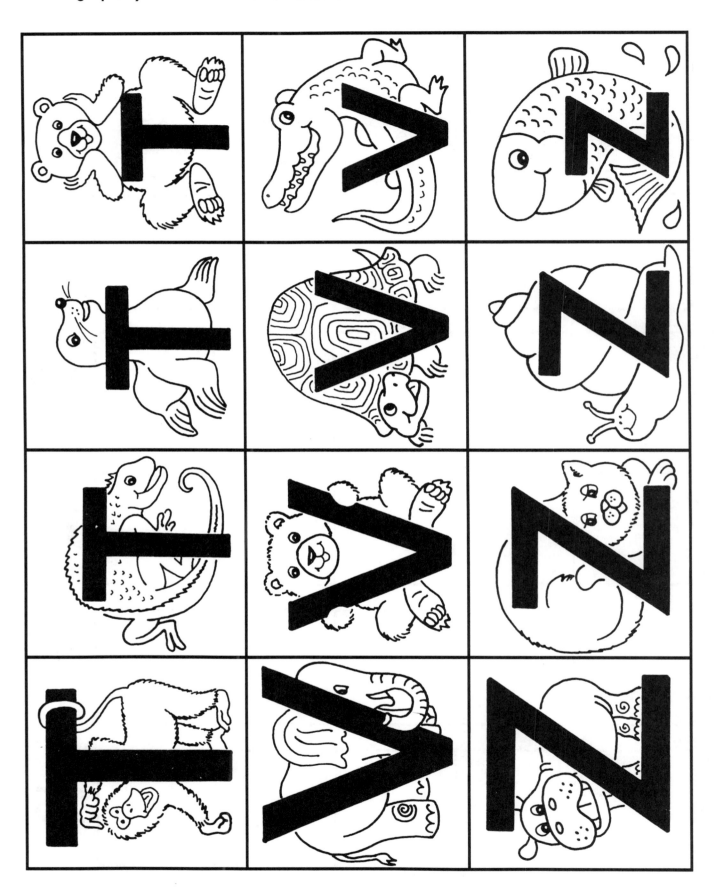

SCIENCE CENTER ACTIVITIES

· · · · · Sensory Letters · · · · ·

Materials Needed: letter stencils, construction paper, texture items (rice for "R," sand or sandpaper for "S," dried leaves for "L," pasta or colored popcorn for "P," cotton balls for "C," and so on), glue, pencils, magnifying glass, scissors

Directions: Provide large letter stencils, construction paper, and corresponding texture materials in a labeled container. Children may select letters to trace on construction paper and then cut them out. Have the children glue textured materials on the letters. When the glue is dry, encourage the child to examine the letters with a magnifying glass. For a wonderful decoration just fasten the "Sensory Letters" on a clothesline and display them in the center.

Variation: When there are enough "Sensory Letters" to spell simple words, encourage children who are interested to make words with them.

· · · · · Alphabet Animal Tree · · · · ·

Materials Needed: nature magazines, project clay (recipe on page 30), scissors, paper, glue, letter-shaped cookie cutters, string, index cards, hole punch, yarn, tree branch, bucket filled with sand, *Chicka Chicka Boom Boom* by Bill Martin, Jr. and John Archambault (Simon and Schuster, 1989).

Directions: How about this festive decoration for the science center—an alphabet tree! It is simple to make; just place a tree branch in a bucket of sand. Now the children can decorate the tree with pictures and letters. Invite the child to find a picture of an animal that she likes and cut it out. Have her glue the picture on an index card. While the glue dries, encourage the child to print the name of the animal on the card and then make a clay letter that corresponds with the animal. Use a pencil to make a small hole at the top of the letter and then set the letter aside to air dry. Punch a hole in the card and thread a piece of yarn through it for hanging the card. When the clay letter is dry, thread a piece of yarn through the hole in the letter and tie the yarn into a loop. Hang the letter near the picture card. The children may also enjoy "reading" the book *Chicka, Chicka, Boom, Boom* in the center.

Variation: Some children may be interested in creating clay animals that match their picture cards on the tree. Display the animals around the base of the tree.

· · · · · Alphabet Plant Match · · · · ·

Materials Needed: fresh flowers and leafy plants, index cards, markers, tape, clean frozen juice cans

Directions: Place each kind of flower (such as rose, daisy, aster, marigold, dandelion) in a juice can. Label each plant by printing its name on an index card. Place these name cards with the flowers. Make a second set of name cards by including simple pictures that resemble the flowers. Invite the child to match the picture/name cards with the actual plants by "reading" the name cards. If the child is making an ABC book, encourage her to print the names of the flowers and plants in her book.

· · · · · Reflect on Letters · · · · ·

Materials Needed: plastic mirrors, plastic or foam letters, letters cut from construction paper

Directions: Encourage the children to explore with mirrors to determine which letters of the alphabet are symmetrical. Introduce the activity during group time by showing a simple paper butterfly to the children. Demonstrate what happens when a mirror is held in the middle of the butterfly (actually is it held on the line of symmetry). In the center, provide only a few letters for the children to investigate with mirrors and then sort into two groups (symmetrical and asymmetrical letters).

Variation: If the children are interested, invite them to work with other objects (blocks, pattern blocks, comb, scissors) to find things that have a line of symmetry.

· · · · · Lots of Letters to Balance · · · · ·

Materials: foam letters, plastic letters, wooden letters, alphabet cereal, letter-shaped pasta, bucket balance, paper, pencil

Directions: Supply various types of letters (foam, wooden, plastic, cereal pieces, pasta) for the children to use for investigating weight. Encourage the children to compare foam letters with plastic letters and so on by filling the buckets of the balance. Which ones are lighter? heavier? How can you fill the buckets to make them the same weight?

Variation: "S" is for sand, "P" is for popcorn, and "B" is for beans. For this investigation, fill identical containers with these materials and label them with the appropriate letter. Encourage the children to investigate the weights of the containers by using the bucket balance. Which one is the lightest? the heaviest?

ART CENTER ACTIVITIES

· · · · · Sponge Letter Prints · · · · ·

Materials Needed: sponge letters, paper, tempera paint, Styrofoam trays, white paper

Directions: We can make interesting designs by printing with sponge letters. Prepare the center materials by pouring small amounts of paint on Styrofoam trays and providing paper and sponge letters. Invite the children to print by dipping the sponges into the paint and pressing the letters against the paper. Be sure they press the letter on the paper several times until they only see " ghost" letters. The children can also print their names and other words or colorful letter prints and designs on the paper.

Variation: Provide a large sheet of mural paper and encourage the children to fill the sheet with prints. When the mural is finished, add splashes of glue and glitter for an extra sparkle!

· · · · · Textured Letter Printing · · · · ·

Materials Needed: old crayons, sandpaper, letter stencils, paper, brayer

Directions: Another unique way to use letters in art is to make sandpaper letters for printing images. To prepare for the activity, cut out letters from sandpaper. Place the gathered materials—paper, crayons, brayer, and sandpaper letters—in a labeled container. Demonstrate to the children how to rub a crayon on the sandpaper letter to cover it with color. When finished, transfer the color by placing the letter *face down* on the paper and roll the brayer across the back of the letter. Press down while moving the brayer back and forth. Pick up the letter to see the results. Place the letter down on a different spot and use the brayer to transfer more color. In the center let the children repeat the process and transfer prints on the construction paper.

· · · · · Story Collage · · · · ·

Materials Needed: magazines, crayons, scissors, paste, paper, stencils, colored construction paper, white construction paper, glitter

Directions: Now we make a collage of pictures and letters. Add some glitter to make the letters sparkle with pizzazz! In the center, encourage the children to clip pictures from magazines and glue them on the paper. Finish the collage by tracing stencils on paper to make letters. Color the letters. For final touch of sparkle, drizzle glue on the paper and then sprinkle glitter on the glue.

· · · · · Finger Paint Letters · · · · ·

Materials Needed: finger paint paper or waxed paper, finger paints or pudding, smock

Directions: Here is a yummy art project that is sure to be a favorite. If pudding is available, have the children wash their hands carefully and then smear pudding on waxed paper. They can print different letters in the pudding before "cleaning" or "licking" their fingers. Perhaps you would like to use finger paints instead of pudding. Just have the children cover the paper with paint and print the letters of the alphabet—hopefully all 26 letters will fit.

· · · · · Button Up the Letters · · · · ·

Materials Needed: buttons or pom-poms, glue, letter stencils, construction paper, scissors, pencil

Directions: Encourage the children to trace a few stencils on their papers and then cut out the letters. To finish the project, have the children glue on buttons or pom-poms to make the letters look unique.

Variation: Perhaps the letters can be used in another center. If the entire alphabet is made the letters can be arranged in alphabetical order. The children can also use the letters to make simple words or label objects with the corresponding initial consonant sounds.

BACKYARD BIRDS
AND OTHER FEATHERED FRIENDS

Take a few minutes to watch the birds that enter your backyard in search of food. Note how they fly, move on the ground by hopping or walking, where they nest, and what foods they prefer to eat when stopping at a bird feeder. Then compare them with birds that live in wooded areas, on ice fields in Antarctica or on ponds. What do all birds have in common? Of course, they are covered with feathers. It is important to remember that not all birds can fly, such as the ostrich and the penguin nor do they feed on the same foods. Many fascinating facts can be shared about birds that live in your region. Take some time to talk about how these birds use their bills and their feet, where they nest, and what foods they eat. This is a perfect opportunity to spend some time observing birds in the neighborhood by taking the children on walking field trips. Visit with people in the community who feed birds and can identify the birds by their calls.

To prepare for this unit of study, change your classroom into an aviary. Using the opaque projector, trace some of the birds pictured on the pattern pages and paint them with tempera paint. Display the birds on the walls along with trees and flowers.

As you set up your centers, be sure to include books about birds for the children to "read" in your library corner. During group time talk about birds or read aloud informative picture books. The following books have useful information:
- Demuth, Patricia Brennan. *Cradles in the Trees: The Story of Bird Nests*. Illus. by Suzanne Barnes. Macmillan. 1994.
- Hirschi, Ron. *What Is a Bird?* Walker and Company, 1987.
- _____. *Where Do Birds Live?* Walker and Company, 1987.

····· The Dramatic Play Center ·····

Change this area into a nature area. Provide bird books, magnifying glass, binoculars, note pads, pencils, chart paper, bird pictures, nest, plastic eggs, feathers, various kinds of bird feeds, markers, cassette tape of bird calls, tape player and recorder, blank cassette tape, camouflage fabric and bird puppets. Each day place different bird tracks near a bird feeder for the children to investigate. Also provide drawing paper and crayons for the children to use.

ACTIVITIES FOR CURRICULUM AREAS

READING & LANGUAGE DEVELOPMENT CENTER ACTIVITIES

• • • • • Backyard Birds Lotto • • • • •

Materials Needed: pattern on page 57, construction paper, scissors, glue, markers, bird identification books

Directions: The fascinating world of birds is right at your fingertips with this lotto set. By matching the delightful pictures children are also strengthening visual discrimination skills. To prepare the materials for this matching game, photocopy the pattern page two times and mount the copies to construction paper. Color as desired. (Please note that the ruby-throated hummingbird and the black-capped chickadee are featured in this set.) Cut apart one set of picture cards as playing cards. The other copy of the pattern page will be the playing board. In the center have the child match the pictures and practice identifying the birds that are featured in this set.

Variation: If the children need to practice matching identical pictures, make three copies of this pattern page and cut apart the pictures. Now the children can sort and match multiple copies of the birds.

• • • • • Concentrating on Birds • • • • •

Materials Needed: pattern on page 58, construction paper, scissors, glue, markers, bird identification books

Directions: This memory match game is easy to play but remember that not all of the birds featured in this game can be seen in backyards. To prepare the game pieces reproduce the pattern page and mount the copy on construction paper. If you prefer large playing cards, enlarge the pattern page before photocopying it. Color the birds as desired and cut apart the cards. *Note:* Refer to a field guide for exact coloration and markings on the birds. Children can play this memory game with partners. To begin play, turn the picture cards *face down* and mix them before arranging the cards in two rows of four each. Each player must turn two cards *face up* to make a match. If a match is made the player keeps the cards. If a match is not made the cards are turned *face down*. Play continues until all matches are made.

· · · · · Matching Sounds Game · · · · ·

Materials Needed: game board pattern on pages 59–60, poster board, scissors, glue, markers, milk jug caps, black permanent marker

Directions: Out in this backyard you can hear more than just bird calls. Invite the children to look closely at the scene and identify the animals shown and the initial consonant sounds in their names. This game board also is perfect for group time discussions. To prepare the materials, transfer the game board pattern to 11" x 17" (279 x 432 mm) copier paper by enlarging the images at 120%. Color the scene and mount it on poster board. Here are some of the initial consonant sounds that are covered in this activity: c-cardinal, b-bee, d-duck, f-feather, g-goldfinch, h-hummingbird, k-killdeer, m-meadowlark, n-nest, r-robin or rocks, s-seed, t-tanager, w-water or woodpecker. Print these letters on the milk jug caps. Now your materials are ready for the children to practice identifying initial consonant sounds. Let the child complete the matches by placing each letter near the corresponding animal/object in the scene.

· · · · · Matching Birds and Babies · · · · ·

Materials Needed: picture card patterns on page 61, scissors, glue, construction paper, markers, bird identification books, nature magazines

Directions: Look at these cute baby birds! Find each bird's mommy to make the match. To prepare the materials, enlarge the pattern cards and then photocopy them. Color the pictures as desired and cut apart the cards. In the center the child may match birds with their young. Be sure to explain to the child that not all young are called chicks. The following names are used: owl–owlets, swan–cygnets, chicken–chicks and penguin–chick. Encourage the children to look through nature magazines and find other pictures of young birds. Invite them to compare and contrast these pictures with the playing cards.

· · · · · Telling Bird Stories · · · · ·

Materials Needed: picture card patterns on page 62–63, scissors, glue, construction paper, markers, bird identification books

Directions: This sorting and sequencing activity causes children to think about how birds perform daily functions. Prepare the materials by duplicating the picture card patterns at 120% or larger and coloring them if desired. Mount the copies on construction paper. Cut apart the pictures and store them in a large envelope. If you prefer to provide an answer key, number each series of cards with a different colored marker. Have the child sort the pictures and then place them in order to tell a story about each bird's activities.

cardinal

goldfinch

Baltimore oriole

robin

hummingbird

chickadee

yellow warbler

woodpecker

blue jay

kestrel

meadowlark

killdeer

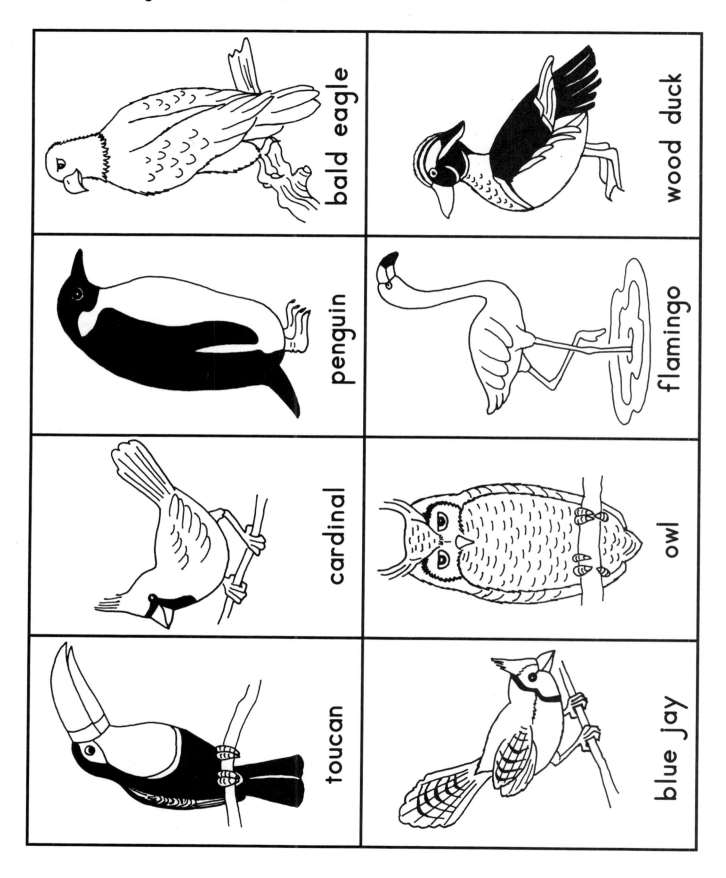

Glue here.

barn owl

owlets

swan

cygnets

chicken

chicks

penguin

chick

Bird Stories Picture Card Patterns

WRITING CENTER ACTIVITIES

· · · · · Seed Words · · · · ·

Materials Needed: letter stencils, bird seed, construction paper, marker, pencil, glue, picture pattern on page 76

Directions: Add a sensory dimension when teaching letters by gluing birdseed on letter cutouts as decoration. To begin the activity, invite the child to trace individual letters or several letters to spell words. *Note:* You may wish to provide a copy of "Facts About Birds" (page 76) for the child to use when printing words. Finish the project by having the child glue seeds on the letters. Set them aside to air dry before displaying them.

· · · · · Printing Bird Names · · · · ·

Materials Needed: lotto board pattern on page 57, manuscript paper, pencil, scissors, glue, laminating material or clear adhesive plastic, watercolor marker, construction paper

Directions: Reproduce a copy of the pattern page and cut apart the pictures. Glue each one on a small piece of manuscript paper. Lightly trace the spelling of the bird's name on the paper. Indicate with a colored mark where the child should start forming each letter. To finish the activity cards, mount the printed copies on construction paper and then laminate them to make them reusable. In the center, have the child select an activity card and practice printing the bird's name. When finished, clean the activity card with a damp cloth. Encourage the child to print other names of birds.

· · · · · Finding Out About Birds' Feet · · · · ·

Materials Needed: patterns on pages 66–67, construction paper, scissors, glue, paper, nature magazines, stapler

Directions: Children will surely notice how birds differ when they compare and contrast the birds' feet. To decorate the center, enlarge the picture card patterns on copier paper and display them. During group time, it is helpful to share information about how birds use their feet. Later in the center the children can record what they have learned in their booklets. To prepare the materials for the center, reproduce the booklet cover for each child and mount it on construction paper. Let the child make the booklet by assembling a few sheets of paper along with the cover. Staple the booklet together. Provide copies of the picture cards (pattern on page 67) for the children to glue in their booklets. It is important for the child to apply what she has learned about birds' feet by determining how the feet differ or are similar. To do this let the child locate a picture of another bird's feet that are similar to one on the picture cards. Have the child glue that picture on the booklet page and tell why this picture was selected.

· · · · · Finding Out About Birds' Bills · · · · ·

Materials Needed: picture card patterns on page 68, construction paper, scissors, glue, paper, nature magazines

Directions: Another important feature of a bird is its bill. This tells so much about how the animal feeds. Children can easily examine pictures of birds to learn about the different kinds of bills. To decorate the center, enlarge the picture card patterns on large sheets of copier paper and display them. In the center, the children can continue to write what they are learning about birds in their booklets "All About Birds" which were started for the activity "Finding Out about Birds' Feet." Let the child glue the pictures of different bills in his booklet. Encourage him to apply what he knows about a bird's bill by locating a picture of another bird with a bill that is similar to one in the picture cards. Have the child glue this picture on the corresponding booklet page and tell why it was selected. The children may also wish to "write" or draw pictures in their booklets about their experiences watching how birds search for food in their backyards.

· · · · · Once Upon a Feather Story · · · · ·

Materials Needed: colorful feathers, paper, construction paper, drawing paper, crayons, pencils, tape, stapler or paper fasteners, tape recorder

Directions: For this activity let the children pretend they have seen the most beautiful birds in the world. Begin the magic by placing a feather in the child's hand. Tell the child about that feather which was dropped by a very special bird. Encourage the child to tell you about this bird and where it traveled. (It may be helpful to record this discussion for the child to refer to later when "writing" the story.) Let the child make a booklet for her story and then "write" and illustrate it. (Some children may wish to dictate their stories to another adult.) When the story is finished, have the child tape the feather(s) in the booklet. Now she has a book to "read" to friends and family members.

All About Birds

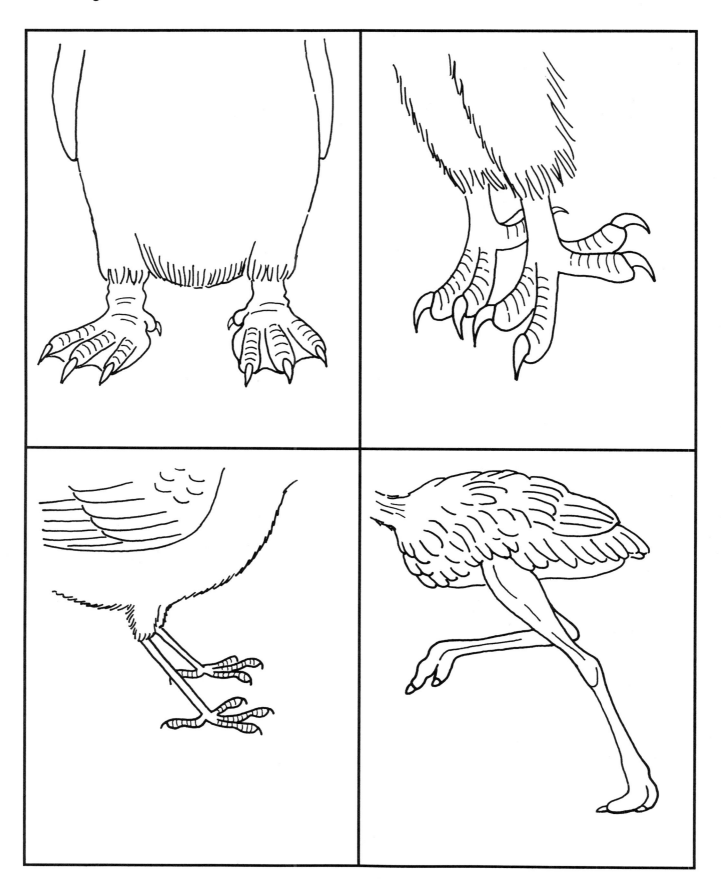

MATH CENTER ACTIVITIES

· · · · · Measure and Compare · · · · ·

Materials Needed: patterns on pages 71, opaque projector, pencil, large sheets of paper, scissors, tempera paint, construction paper, bulletin board paper

Directions: Just how many hummingbirds tall is a great blue heron? Are your young learners taller than the heron? These questions can be investigated as your students work with patterns of these birds. To prepare the materials for the activity, reproduce about 20 copies of the hummingbird and mount them on construction paper. Cut out the birds. Knowing that the great blue heron is 4 ft. or 1.2 m tall, use the opaque projector to enlarge the heron to this size on bulletin board paper. After tracing the outline of the bird, paint it with tempera paint so the children will know it is a great blue heron. Display the bird on a wall close to the floor. Provide the children with opportunities to compare their heights with the bird's height. Let each child work with a partner and measure the heron's height with the small hummingbird cutouts. The tiny hummingbird is truly another amazing animal when compared with the great blue heron.

Variation: Invite the children to measure their heights with the hummingbird cutouts to find out how much larger they are than these birds.

· · · · · Feather Measure · · · · ·

Materials Needed: feathers (several different lengths), string, scissors

Directions: For this activity have the child arrange a selection of feathers from longest to shortest or vice versa. When the child is finished with the task, ask him to decide which feather is the shortest and which one is the longest. Instead of arranging the feathers in seriation have the child randomly select a feather and cut a piece of string that is the same length. When finished let the child use the string to measure the other feathers and then sort them into groups—feathers that are shorter, longer and the same size.

Variation: Find several feathers that are the same length. Invite the child to measure a partner's height with those feathers.

Colorful Egg Patterns

Materials Needed: two egg cartons, stapler, scissors, pattern on page 72, plastic eggs (several of each color), markers

Directions: Egg cartons and plastic eggs can be wonderful teaching tools for repeat patterns. Just cut off the lids of two egg cartons and staple them together to provide 12 cavities in a row. Reproduce the patterns on page 72 two or three times to make several task cards. Using markers that correspond with the plastic eggs, color the egg shapes with an ABAB, AABB, or ABBA pattern for children to follow as they place plastic eggs in the egg cartons. Another suggestion, let the children work with two different sizes of plastic eggs when continuing repeat patterns by creating your own task cards for the children to follow.

Cover Up and Count

Materials Needed: picture pattern on page 73, construction paper, linking cubes or round counters

Directions: How many counters are needed to cover up the penguin? What size is the penguin if fewer counters are needed to cover it? For children to investigate these questions, photocopy the penguin at 70%, 100% and 125%. Mount the copies on construction paper. Invite the child to cover the medium-sized penguin with math counters. When finished, have him count the pieces to find out how many are used to cover the penguin. Encourage the child to select another penguin and find out if more or less counters are used to cover the bird. When finished, group the counters in a pile. Does the pile have fewer counters than the first pile?

Fill 'Em Up with Birdseed

Materials Needed: birdseed, identical plastic cups, different sized plastic containers, large tub, picture card patterns on page 72

Directions: Investigating the volume of containers can easily be handled with birdseed and several identical plastic cups. Reproduce the pattern page that shows four tasks for the child to complete. Set the task cards along with the gathered materials in a large tub. *Note:* Beforehand, locate various plastic containers that hold two, three, four, or five plastic cups of birdseed. Encourage the child to experiment with different sizes of containers by filling them with cupfuls of birdseed. When the child knows which container holds only two cups of birdseed, have her place the task card next to that container. Encourage the child to continue the process until all containers have been identified.

Colorful Egg Patterns

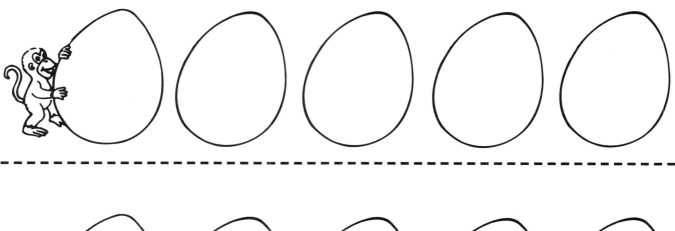

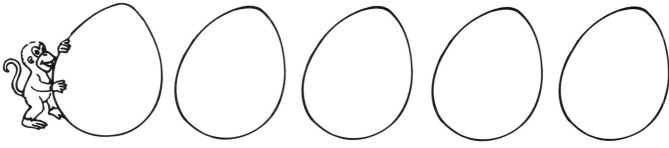

Fill 'Em Up with Birdseed Patterns

SCIENCE CENTER ACTIVITIES

· · · · · Sprouting Seeds · · · · ·

Materials Needed: bucket balance, clean margarine containers with lids (all the same size), different kinds of birdseed in separate containers, sponges, water, magnifying glass, small scoops, large plastic tub

Directions: Here is the scoop! We will find out exactly what birdseed is. To prepare for the activity, gather the materials and place the items in a large tub. In the center, encourage the children to investigate different packages of birdseed. Be sure the children notice that the bag which is a mixture of seeds contains seeds that are also supplied in other containers separately. The children may also investigate weights by filling one plastic container with thistle seed, another identical container with sunflower seeds, and so on. Do these containers have the same weight? Have the child use the bucket balance to find out the answer. When she is finished making observations about the birdseed, have the child place a few seeds on a damp sponge and set it aside for a couple of days. Keep the sponge moist and encourage the child to watch for germination.

· · · · · Observing Pet Birds · · · · ·

Materials Needed: pet bird in cage, magnifying glass, birdseed, picture card patterns on pages 76–77

Directions: By watching a pet bird, children can make observations about how it eats, drinks water and preens its feathers. Set the pet bird on a table along with a magnifying glass and some birdseed. (Include a copy of the upper left-hand picture from the science investigation pattern page to remind the child about the investigation.) Have the child watch the bird for a few minutes and then share what he observed. Give the child a copy of the "Facts About Birds" and have him work with a partner as he locates the bird's body parts.

Variation: You may also wish to reproduce the pattern page to make a lotto game.

· · · · · Home in a Nest · · · · ·

Materials Needed: old bird's nests, twigs, grass, leaves, magnifying glass, mud, picture card patterns on pages 57 and 77, books on birds, construction paper, glue

Directions: A bird's nest certainly is a fascinating structure. For this activity let your young learners carefully study a few old nests that are brought into the classroom. It is important to prepare the nests by spraying them with a disinfectant before allowing the children to touch them. To prepare for the activity gather common materials that birds use to build nests and also make a copy of the science investigation card (upper right-hand corner) for this activity along with the lotto board pattern page. Cut apart the pictures and mount them on construction paper. In the center, have the children carefully examine the nests to determine how they are similar or different and what materials were used to make them. *Note:* If it is possible try to provide nests made by different kinds of birds for the children to examine. The investigations are then much more interesting. This activity can be extended by letting the children look for pictures of nests that are made by the birds featured in the picture cards. Have the child mark the page in the book with the corresponding picture card. It is important to remember that not all of the birds featured on the pattern page build nests in trees. For example, the killdeer may place some twigs in a bowl-shaped hollow in the sandy ground before laying its eggs.

Variation: If you know the location of several nests, take the children on a walking field trip and visit the nesting sites. Be sure to caution the children not to touch the nests. This ensures that the nests will not be abandoned by their owners.

· · · · · Investigating Earthworms · · · · · ·

Materials Needed: earthworms, dirt, plastic container, magnifying glass, clean Styrofoam tray, paper towels, paper, pattern page 77, paper, pencils or crayons

Directions: How does an earthworm move? Which bird feeds on earthworms? To prepare for the activity, photocopy the science instruction card (lower left-hand corner) and place it with the other gathered materials. In the center, provide healthy earthworms for the children to closely examine on Styrofoam trays. Encourage the children to touch the earthworms and describe how they feel. When they are finished with their observations, have them draw pictures and "write" about what they observed.

· · · · · Pinecone Feeders · · · · ·

Materials Needed: birdseed, peanut butter (smooth), pinecones, plastic knives, picture card pattern on page 77, string

Directions: To make these nutritional bird snacks, mix a lot of birdseed in some peanut butter. Reproduce the picture card pattern to show a completed pinecone feeder. Cut out the card and place it with the prepared birdseed mixture and pinecones. Have the child spread the birdseed mixture on the pinecone. Tie a piece of string to hang the feeder. Now it is snack time for the birds in your backyard!

Facts About Birds

eye

throat

feather

feet

leg

nest

eggs

crown

bill

body

tail

wing

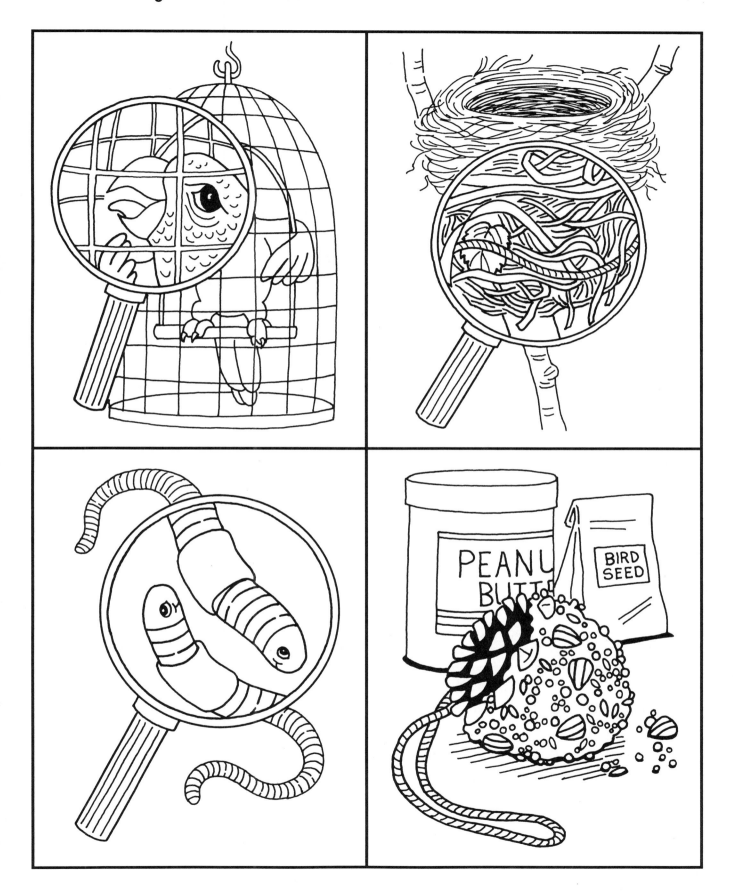

ART CENTER ACTIVITIES

• • • • • Feather Art • • • • •

Materials Needed: feathers, three Styrofoam trays, tempera paints (red, yellow and blue), newsprint, plastic spoons, optional—bird sounds on cassette tape and tape player

Directions: Let your imagination fly while listening to bird calls. Spread tempera paint on each tray with a plastic spoon. Invite the child to paint with feathers by dipping them in the paints and then stroking the paper with them. Allow the painting to dry before displaying it.

• • • • • Bird Collage • • • • •

Materials Needed: nature magazines and calendars that feature birds, feathers, birdseed, glue, scissors, construction paper, nature items (twigs, grasses, flowers)

Directions: Gather the necessary items for creating collages and store them in a labeled bin. Have the children clip pictures of birds and related items and then glue them on construction paper. Nature items may also be included in the collage with the pictures.

• • • • • Building Nests • • • • •

Materials Needed: old bird nests (treated with disinfectant spray), twigs, mud, grass, straw and other building materials

Directions: Set the natural materials along with the bird nests on a table. Encourage the children to build nests with the gathered materials.

• • • • • Dip 'n' Color Eggs • • • • •

Materials Needed: hard-boiled eggs, egg coloring dyes, spoons, plastic cups, sponges, food coloring, vinegar, paint smocks

Directions: It is always fun to color eggs. Follow the directions on the dye package for coloring the eggs. Show the children how they can dip half of an egg in one color and then the other half in a second color. If the child would like the egg to be speckled, dip a piece of sponge in a food coloring and vinegar solution and then dab the coloring on the egg. Display the eggs when finished.

• • • • • Seed Designs • • • • •

Materials Needed: seeds, glue, paper or cardboard, pencil, large flat tray

Directions: Wonderful designs can be created with seeds. Encourage the children to draw designs and then glue a variety of seeds in place to show the shapes and details. *Note:* It is helpful to store the seeds in easy-to-pour containers. Collect the seeds that do not adhere to the board in a flat tray.

BEES AND SWEET TREATS

One very fascinating insect is the honey bee. This small remarkable animal works hard and lives a short life in a community that may include thousands of others in the colony. Children are intrigued by how bees live and work. Using the materials in this theme, share facts about bees and their products. Even though people eat honey as food, there are other products that also could be featured—candles and lipsticks made from beeswax. As you highlight how beneficial the bee is to people, be sure to remember that the bee has an important role in the fertilization of a flower. Each time it lands on a flower, some pollen clings to its body or is brushed off as the bee collects nectar. Unbeknownst to the bee, this process of transferring pollen from plant to plant is crucial to the plant's life cycle.

Change your classroom into a special learning environment about bees. To do this, create giant-size wall decorations by enlarging bee patterns on bulletin board paper. You might like to add scenery pieces to enhance your wildlife scene.

As you set up your centers, be sure to include books about bees for the children to read in your library corner. During group time talk about bees or read aloud informative picture books. The following books have useful information:
- Fischer-Nagel, Heiderose and Andreas. *Life of the Honeybee.* Carolrhoda, 1986.
- Hogan, Paula Z. *The Honeybee.* Raintree Childrens Books, 1979.

····· The Dramatic Play Center ·····

Transform this area into a natural habitat for bees. Perhaps you know a beekeeper who can loan an empty hive to your class for a short time. Be imaginative! Fill the center with wonderful props to encourage your young learners to be creative during their play. Some children may enjoy wearing "Buzzing Bee Hats" which are yellow headbands with black pipe cleaner antennae. The children can finish the bands by drawing five eyes on each one. Another interesting prop is a bee stick puppet. To make these puppets, use white paper, black and yellow paints, and construction paper for wings and legs. With a little imagination, create your bee puppets and then attach craft sticks for moving them. In one area of the center set up a "Honey Studio." Display honey products (in plastic containers) and pictures of bees. Also provide paper, pencils and plastic bees (optional). If it is possible play nature music for the children to hear while in the center area.

ACTIVITIES FOR CURRICULUM AREAS

READING & LANGUAGE DEVELOPMENT CENTER ACTIVITIES

· · · · · Bees and Treats Lotto Game · · · · ·

Materials Needed: lotto board pattern on page 83, construction paper, glue, scissors, markers

Directions: This activity certainly is "buzzing" with new words to learn and match. Before preparing the materials decide how the children will complete the lotto game. If the children are matching pictures, make two photocopies of the pattern page. However, if the children are ready to match labeled pictures with words, provide a lotto board that only shows the words. To do this, cover the pictures before making a copy of the board. (Refer to pattern page 16 to see how the board should look.) For the playing cards make a copy of the pattern page with the pictures shown. When finished making the photocopies, mount them on construction paper and cut apart one photocopy to make the playing cards. Color the pictures as desired and set the materials in the center. Now the children can match and not be "stuck" on sweet treats and bees.

· · · · · Five Busy Bees Poem · · · · ·

Materials Needed: rhyme on page 84, large construction paper, watercolor markers, laminating material, bee pattern on page 95, construction paper, tape recorder, blank cassette tape

Directions: Five bees will be buzzing as the children work with this finger play. To make the finger puppets, duplicate five bees at a smaller size and mount them on small construction paper strips that are rolled into bands for wearing on the fingers. Reproduce the poem by enlarging it to fit on 11" x 17" (279 x 432 mm) copier paper. Laminate the copy. For the activity, provide a recording of the poem for the children to hear while showing the actions with finger puppets. When the children are finished listening to the poem, have them circle the "Bb" and other designated letters with watercolor markers. For cleanup, use a damp paper towel to remove the markings.

• • • • • Busy Bee Rhymes • • • • •

Materials Needed: patterns on pages 85–86, construction paper, scissors, markers, glue

Directions: For this activity just rhyme sets of three pictures to be as busy as bees. To prepare the materials, make photocopies of the pattern pages. Mount the playing board and the rhyming pictures on construction paper and color them as desired. You may wish to laminate the materials for durability (optional). When finished, cut out the rhyming pictures to make the playing cards. Now your game is complete. In the center, invite the child to sort the pictures that rhyme and arrange them in sets on the board.

• • • • • Where Is Bee? • • • • •

Materials Needed: picture cards on page 87, construction paper, scissors, glue

Directions: This bee certainly is busy moving around the hive. Look carefully so you can answer the question "Where is Bee?" To prepare the picture cards reproduce them at 100% or enlarge them to fit on 11" x 17" (279 x 432 mm) paper. Mount the copy on construction paper and cut apart the picture cards. Using the picture cards, have the child work with a partner and describe the location of the bee in relation to the hive. Some children may be ready to identify pairs of cards that have opposite meanings, such as on and off, above and below.

Variation: If appropriate, the materials can be used for a matching activity by making a second copy of the picture cards and then the child can match identical pictures.

• • • • • Bee Pogs Game • • • • •

Materials Needed: picture patterns on page 88, scissors, glue, markers, construction paper

Directions: For this activity, use the materials for a matching game. To do this, reproduce two copies of the pattern page (you may wish to enlarge the pictures when copying them) and mount them on construction paper. Cut apart the pictures. Select the pictures for the children to match. If appropriate let the child play a memory match game with a partner. To begin play turn the picture cards *face down* and mix them before arranging the cards in two rows. Each player must turn two cards *face up* to make a match. If a match is made the player keeps the cards. If a match is not made the cards are turned *face down*. Play continues until all matches are made. Instead of a memory match game, have the children match picture to picture or labeled picture with word. To make the word pogs, cover the pictures before making the second photocopy of the pattern page.

Bees and Treats

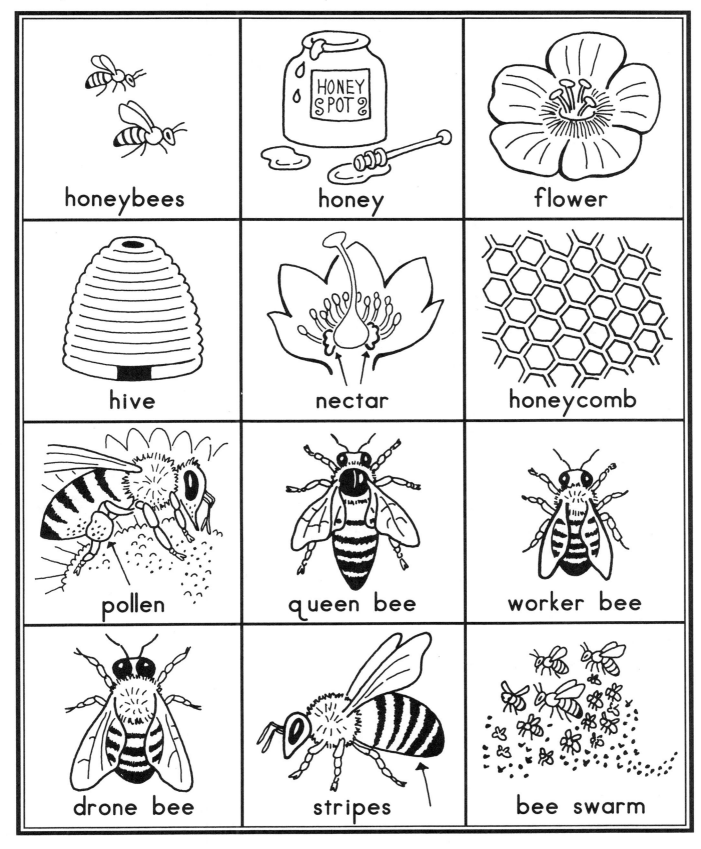

honeybees	honey	flower
hive	nectar	honeycomb
pollen	queen bee	worker bee
drone bee	stripes	bee swarm

Five Busy Honeybees

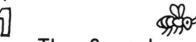

Five busy honeybees were resting in the sun.

1

The first bee said, "Let us have some fun."

The second bee said, "Where shall it be?"

2

The third bee said, "Up in the honey tree."

3

The fourth bee said, "Let's make some honey sweet."

The fifth bee said, "With pollen on our feet."

4

The five little busy bees sang their buzzing tune,

As they worked in the beehive all that afternoon.

5

Bzzzzzzz!   Bzzzzzzz!

—Adapted from Louise Binder Scott

 # Busy Bee Rhymes

Busy Bee Rhymes Pictures

 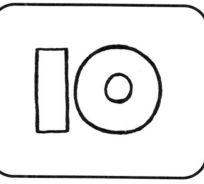 

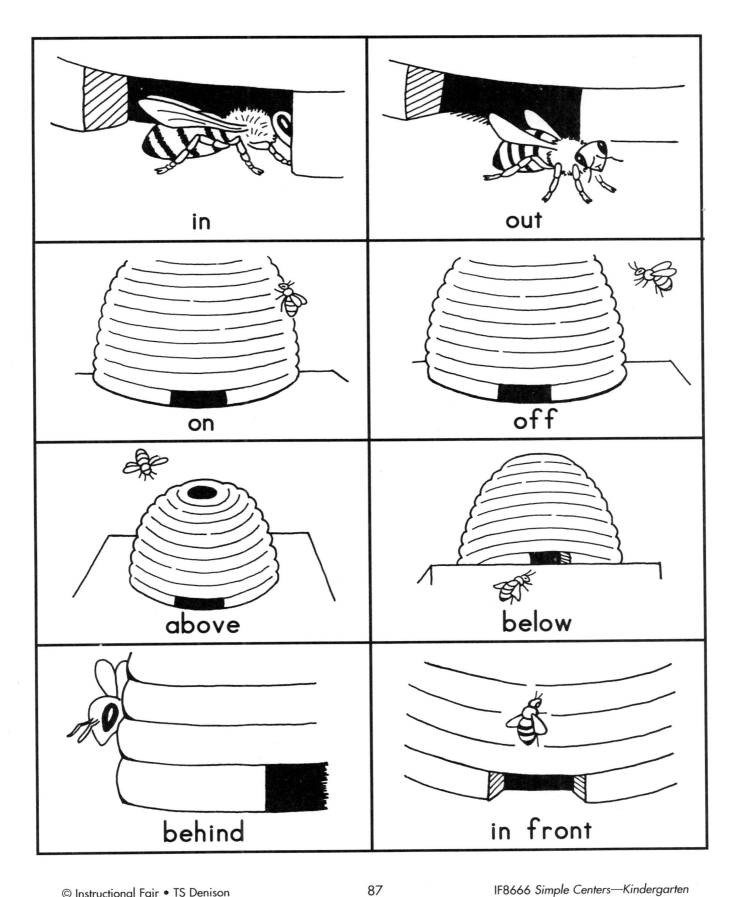

in

out

on

off

above

below

behind

in front

WRITING CENTER ACTIVITIES

· · · · · Buzzing Words in the Honey Tree · · · · ·

Materials Needed: bee pattern on page 91, hive pattern on page 95, construction paper, markers, scissors, glue, tree branch, paper clips, hole punch, bucket with sand

Directions: Decorate your writing center with a tree filled with new words that "buzz" around a hive. To prepare the materials, reproduce the beehive and enough bee patterns for displaying words the children are learning. (The children may also enjoy "reading" their names on the bees.) Mount the bees and beehive on construction paper and cut out the shapes. Color as desired. Locate a tree branch and place it upright in a bucket of sand. Now the cutouts are ready for the children to print words and the letter "Bb" on them. To hang the beehive and bees in the "tree," use opened paper clips that resemble an "S."

Variations: You may wish to make rebus pictures for some of the words by cutting out the pictures on a photocopy of the "Bees and Treats" pattern on page 83. For a sorting activity, have the children group the bees according to the first letter of the word printed on each one.

· · · · · A Taste of Honey · · · · ·

Materials Needed: honey, clean spoons, paper, colored pencils, chart paper, picture cards on page 83, construction paper

Directions: Here is an opportunity for children to taste honey and write about it. Reproduce a copy of the "Bees and Treats" pattern page by enlarging it to fit on 11" x 17" (279 x 432 mm) paper. Display the chart in the center for the children to view. After the child tastes the honey, encourage her to write and draw pictures about honey.

Variation: If appropriate, have the child "read" books to gather more information about honey and then "write" about it.

· · · · · A Colorful "Bb" · · · · ·

Materials Needed: large black construction paper, white chalk, yellow tissue paper, index cards, scissors, paper cutter, marker, black paper scraps, pencil, paste

Directions: This "berry" delightful yellow "B" certainly pleases the young learner. With minimal preparation the materials are ready for making colorful "B"s. To get started, outline a large bold-shaped "Bb" on a sheet of black construction paper with white chalk, one for each child. Make a set of word cards for each child by printing dashed-shaped letters for the words "yellow" and "black" on separate cards. Using the paper cutter, cut a large number of 3" (76 mm) tissue paper squares. In the center, have the child roll the tissue paper into round balls or berries and glue them on the "Bb." When finished, have the child trace over the letters on the word cards and glue a few yellow berries near the word "yellow" and a piece of black construction paper near the word "black." The black and yellow "B"s add so much color to the writing center. You may wish to use them as part of the classroom decorations.

· · · · · Honeybee Recipes · · · · ·

Materials Needed: recipe pattern on page 91, pencils, cookbooks

Directions: If you were a bee how would you prepare your favorite food dish? Even though bees do not cook, young learners may be able to think about different ways to use honey when making foods. These "favorite food dishes" can be recorded on the special recipe cards. Just provide a reproduced copy of the pattern page for each child. If available, share cookbooks that offer different ways for using honey in food preparation.

· · · · · My Honey Story · · · · ·

Materials Needed: Winnie the Pooh story books, pencils, paper, crayons, colored pencils, markers

Directions: During group time share stories about Winnie the Pooh and how he loves honey. Select a story and read only part of it to the children. Encourage the children to tell how they think the story should end. In the center, have each child write an ending for the story and draw a picture.

Variation: The children may have other stories about honey and bees that they would like to write. Encourage them to use the provided materials to make their own books.

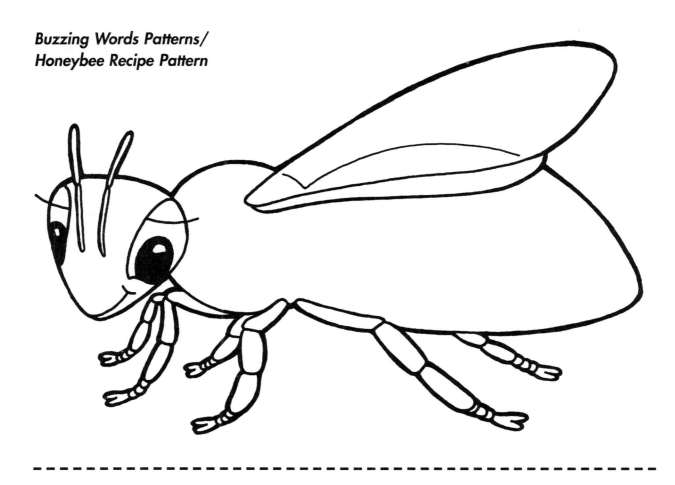

- -

Math Center Activities

· · · · · Beehive Math · · · · ·

Materials Needed: patterns on page 94, construction paper, scissors, markers, five spring clothespins, glue

Directions: Listen for a buzzing of numbers as children count the bees resting on these hives. Before you begin to prepare the activity materials, decide which sets of numbers are appropriate for the children to count—for example, sets of 5 to 10 or sets of 10 to 15. Reproduce five beehives that are enlarged to fit on 11" x 17" (279 x 432 mm) paper and enough bees to make the sets. Mount the beehives on construction paper and glue a predetermined number of bees on each hive. Finish the preparation by printing a corresponding numeral on each clothespin. Color as desired and laminate the sets for durability (optional).

Variation: If appropriate, group the bees on the hives before gluing them. For example, if the children are working with the concepts of one more or two more, arrange the bees on the hive to show these concepts. For instance, the sets could be 3 and 1, 4 and 1, 5 and 1, and so on, or 3 and 2, 4 and 2, 5 and 2 and so on.

· · · · · Buzzing with Patterns · · · · ·

Materials Needed: construction paper (black and yellow), pattern on page 95, paper cutter

Directions: Here is an interesting task. Have your young learners buzzing with these black and yellow striped patterns. To prepare the materials, cut the paper into 3½" x 1" (89 x 25 mm) strips, providing approximately 20 strips in each color. Photocopy the activity card pattern by enlarging the top half of the pattern page at 150% to fit on copier paper. Make four copies of the card pattern and mount them on construction paper. Glue a few strips on each activity card to begin a repeat pattern. In the center encourage the child to finish the pattern by placing the paper strips on the table near the activity card.

Variation: Check out your pattern blocks. Find the triangle, square, and hexagon. Show the children a picture of a honeycomb. Have them identify which shape the bees use to make their honeycomb by selecting the appropriate pattern blocks. Each child can also build a "honeycomb" by working with the hexagons to create a tessellating pattern. This is possible because hexagons, squares, or triangles can be arranged to cover the entire surface. You will notice no spaces between the shapes.

· · · · · Measuring with Bees · · · · ·

Materials Needed: patterns on page 95, construction paper, scissors, glue, pencils

Directions: What is 3 bees tall in the classroom? 4 bees tall? 5 bees tall? The children can hunt for items to answer these or other questions or perhaps build structures with blocks to obtain these heights. Before they begin measuring, supply 10 copies of the bee pattern mounted on construction paper and cut them out. Color them as desired and laminate for durability (optional). In the center, have the children find objects that match the lengths indicated on the picture cards.

· · · · · Making a Bee · · · · ·

Materials Needed: play clay, golf tees, straight pins, pipe cleaners, construction paper, craft sticks, instruction cards on page 96, scissors, glue

Directions: Children can learn to identify and count the parts of a bee's body by constructing a model. Supply play clay, two golf tees, three straight pins along with paper and craft sticks for each child. Photocopy the instruction card pattern and mount it on construction paper. Laminate the cards for durability (optional). Make a model for the children to view as they construct their own models. Follow the instructions on the cards. To make the wings, cut out wing shapes from construction paper and glue them to pieces of craft sticks (use scissors to cut them in half).

· · · · · "Bee" Alert Game · · · · ·

Materials Needed: cereal that resembles honeycombs, dice, waxed paper, clean ice cube tongs, counting board pattern on page 47

Directions: Gather, count and "bee" alert for a tasty treat. To prepare for this game, purchase cereal that resembles a honeycomb and store the cereal in a small plastic container. Locate a pair of tongs that the children can use to pick up the cereal pieces. Make two photocopies of the counting board pattern. To begin the game, encourage the child to find a partner. Give each player a piece of waxed paper to cover the counting board. (This ensures that the cereal game pieces can be eaten later.) Decide how many pieces of cereal each player should collect. Play begins when the first player rolls a die and places the corresponding number of cereal pieces on the counting board. Of course the player must use the tongs to pick up the cereal pieces. Have the players continue taking turns until both counting boards are filled. For additional counting practice, each player must announce how many pieces of cereal are on the board at the end of each turn. If you would like to add a "wild card" element to the game, direct the players to **not** add any cereal pieces to the counting board if the number 6 is rolled. This number stands for "bee warning" because a bee has six legs. When this game is finished the children may either play another game or eat some of the cereal for a treat.

94

Buzzing with Patterns

- -

Measuring with Bees Patterns

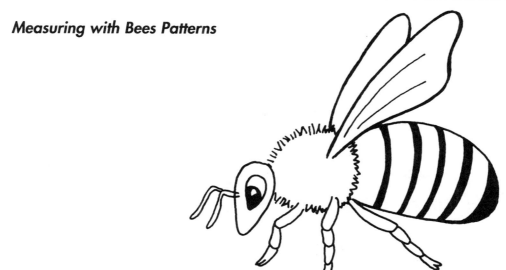

? = 🐜🐜	? = 🐜🐜🐜🐜
? = 🐜🐜🐜	? = 🐜🐜🐜🐜🐜

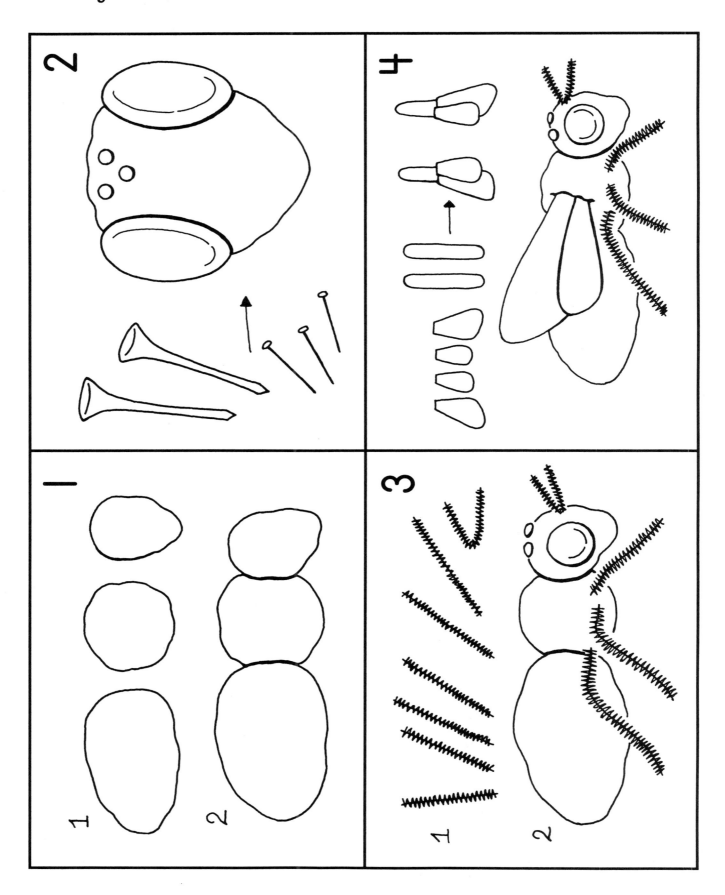

SCIENCE CENTER ACTIVITIES

· · · · · Honeycomb Observations · · · · ·

Materials Needed: honey, honeycomb, magnifying glass, trays, pattern on page 99

Directions: Be careful with this "sticky" investigation. If possible, obtain a piece of honeycomb and some honey for the children to closely examine. Photocopy the science investigation card for this activity. (Select the card in the upper right-hand corner of the page.) In the science center pour some honey on one tray and set the honeycomb on a separate tray. Place the science investigation card with the magnifying glass near the trays. Encourage the child to examine the honeycomb, looking for honey that is encased.

Variation: If possible, supply other natural items such as an old beehive for the children to closely examine. Children enjoy using a flashlight and a magnifying glass to study these fascinating hives. You may wish to have the children also examine beeswax candles.

· · · · · Honey Drops and Magnifiers · · · · ·

Materials Needed: honey, clean Styrofoam trays, water, wooden building blocks, newspaper, waxed paper, magnifying lens, pattern on page 99

Directions: Is honey a liquid? Will it move like water? Young learners can investigate these questions and also discover how a drop of honey does act like a magnifying lens. Gather the recommended items and place them in a storage container. Photocopy the science investigation card for this activity. (Select the card in the upper left-hand corner of the page.) In the center encourage the child to build a steep ramp with the blocks and then place the tray on it. Now place a drop of honey and a drop of water on the end of the tray closest to the top of the ramp. Watch what happens. The child will observe how the drop of honey and the drop of water change and the liquids run down the tray. Which one wins the race? For the second part of the investigation, have the child place a drop of honey and a drop of water on waxed paper which is resting on newspaper. Look at the print through the drops. Is the print larger in size? Perhaps the young learners have other questions about honey they might like to investigate. For example, "Will drops of honey and water disappear (evaporate) if left to air dry overnight?"

· · · · · Looking for Pollen · · · · ·

Materials Needed: fresh flowers that have large flower parts (pistil, stamen), magnifying glass, paper, colored pencils or crayons, paper towel, cotton swabs, pattern on page 99

Directions: Where is pollen found on the flower? Where is nectar made? Provide fresh flowers that have a large pistil and prominent stamens for the children to closely examine. For example, the parts of the lily flower are easy to identify. Also provide a photocopy of the science investigation card for this activity. (Select the card in the lower left-hand corner of the page.) Place the gathered materials on a tray. For your information: Look for pollen on the stamen (anther). It can be collected on a cotton swab. Nectar is harder to find. This sweet liquid is produced by glands called nectaries which are located at the base of the pistil.

Variation: If appropriate, some children may be interested in drawing a flower or the parts of the flower. Encourage them to "write" a sentence about what they learned.

· · · · · The Life Cycle of a Bee · · · · ·

Materials Needed: picture cards pattern on page 100, construction page, scissors, glue

Directions: This sequencing activity causes children to think about the bee's life cycle. Prepare the materials by reproducing the picture card patterns and coloring them as desired. Mount the copies on construction paper. Cut apart the pictures and store them in a large envelope. If you prefer to provide an answer key, number the series of cards with a colored marker. Have the child arrange the pictures in order and tell a partner a story about the activities shown.

· · · · · Comparing Weights · · · · ·

Materials Needed: three different-sized jars of honey, bucket balance, construction paper, other items to weigh, pattern on page 99

Directions: Which jar is the heaviest? the lightest? Set up an investigation about weights for the children. Provide a bucket balance and math counters along with a copy of the instruction card. (Select the card in the lower right-hand corner of the page.) Encourage the children to compare the jars of honey by using the bucket balance. The children may weigh each jar while filling the other bucket of the balance with math counters to offset the mass of the honey jar. When finished, count the math counters and record the results. The results for each honey jar can be compared and then the children can determine which jar is the heaviest or the lightest.

98

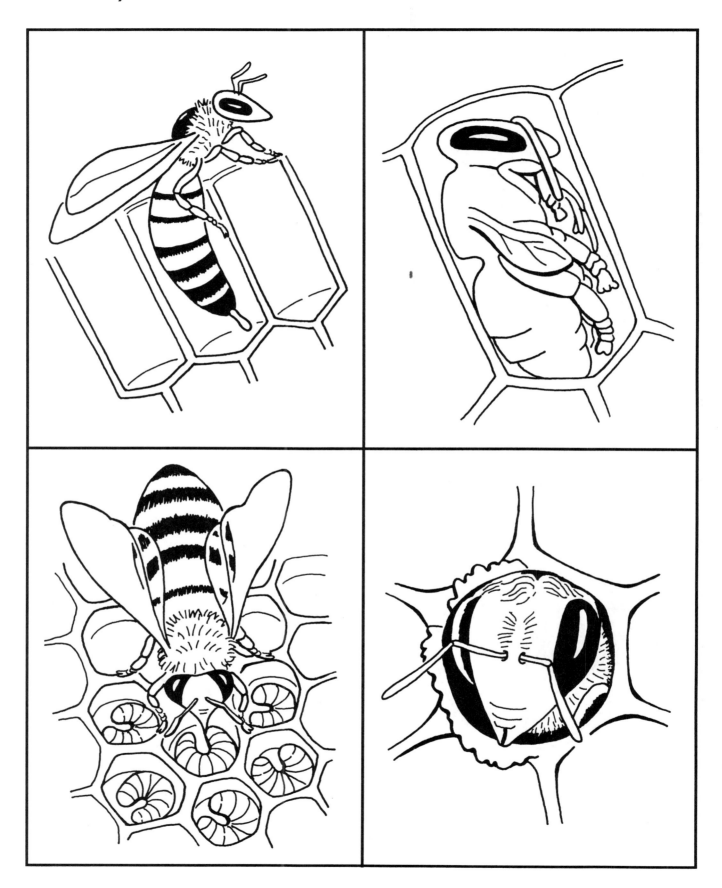

ART CENTER ACTIVITIES

• • • • • Bee Colors • • • • •

Materials Needed: yellow and black tempera paint, paintbrushes, smock, paper, art easel

Directions: Colorful swirls, interesting line patterns, or black and yellow pictures will certainly brighten your art corner. Encourage the child to create a picture with the two paint colors provided.

• • • • • Honeycomb Necklace • • • • •

Materials Needed: elastic string, several large needles, cereal shaped like honeycomb, storage container

Directions: Cut string into 12" (305 mm) lengths. Thread a large needle and then tie one end of the string to it. Place the cereal in a small plastic container. With the materials, invite the child to string cereal to create this tasty necklace.

• • • • • Bee Prints • • • • •

Materials Needed: black and yellow finger paints, finger paint paper, smock, wide-toothed combs

Directions: For this activity the children will certainly be buzzing as they make a picture and a print from the picture. To get them started, place a dab of each color on the paper. Invite the child to spread the paint on the paper and then draw interesting pictures with a fingertip or use the comb to create designs. When the picture is finished, place a second piece of paper on top of the paint. With light pressure smoothen the paper to transfer a copy of the design. Peel the top sheet of the paper off the painting. Now there are two pictures.

Variation: Here is another idea for bee print pictures. Just dip your finger in the paint and then make a print on the paper. Continue until the paper is full of prints. Use a marker to add additional details and watch how these colorful bees fly across the paper.

• • • • • Papier-Mâché Hive • • • • •

Materials Needed: newspaper, glue, water, plastic bowl, paintbrush, scissors, balloons, tan tempera paint

Directions: Children will enjoy changing a balloon into a beehive. To prepare the materials, cut newspaper into long thin strips. Pour a small amount of glue into a bowl and add water to make a thin glue mixture. Inflate a balloon for each child. Set the materials on a table in the center and the balloons in a storage container. To make the beehive, let the child brush glue on half of the balloon and then place strips of newspaper on the prepared surface. Be sure the strips of newspaper overlap. Repeat the process for the other half of the balloon. Set it aside to dry before adding the second and third layers of newspaper. *Note:* This project can also be a cooperative project by having the children work with partners. To finish the project, let the child paint the hive with tan paint. When the paint is dry, add the final details—bees. The child may either paint bees on the hive or cut out bees from magazines and glue them in place. These hives certainly can be used to decorate the classroom as a learning environment about bees.

• • • • • Clay Bees • • • • •

Materials Needed: yellow and black project clay (recipe on page 60), index cards, yellow construction paper, plastic knives, marker, black chenille stems, index cards

Directions: Watch out for giant-sized bees resting in the art center! Young artists can create the bees with project clay and chenille stems. Prepare the clay by following the recipe provided and then coloring enough black and yellow clay for each child. In the center let the child create bees with the clay. To identify who made the bee, have the child sign a name card (index card folded in half like a tent). If the child has a name for the bee, include it on the name card.

EARTH-FRIENDLY CARE

This theme offers children an opportunity to learn many acts of kindness toward the environment. Why it is important to reduce, recycle and reuse materials that have been produced. By encouraging children to act "earthwise" at home and at school, we are teaching children to take responsibility in small ways and make a difference in improving the environment. Earth Day is April 28 but this day can happen everyday if we make an effort to recycle materials—newspaper, tin, glass, and aluminum cans. These materials are 100% recyclable! The plastic waste stream is a more complicated issue, but some plastics are not being reused in new products. It is important to find out how recycling is handled in your community. Perhaps the children could take walking field trips to various locations to investigate what people are doing in the community to improve the environment.

As you set up your centers, be sure to include books about recycling, conserving energy, landfills, natures' recyclers, and related occupations for the children to "read" in your library corner. During group time talk about environmental awareness (reduction, reuse and recycle) and being "earthwise" or read aloud informative picture books. The following books have useful information:

- Fleming, Denise. Where *Once There Was a Wood*. Henry Holt & Company, 1996.
- Lowery, Linda and Marybeth Lorbiecki. *Earthwise at home*. Carolrhoda Books, 1993.
- _____. *Earthwise at school*. Carolrhoda Books, 1993.

····· The Dramatic Play Center ·····

Transform this center for travel experiences. In one part of the center create a travel agency. Some children can be vacationers or tourists while others can be travel agents. Provide brochures from agencies, play money for tickets, charts for different ways to travel, and more. To help children realize that we must preserve the breathtaking beauty of Earth by keeping the air and water clean, invite them to "see" the world. Just imagine the places they could visit. In a separate location within the center area set up a large dryer or washing machine box or tent as the vacation location. Inside of the structure display posters and pictures from magazines to create vacation spots. Be sure to include empty wrappers, clean plastic soda bottles, and other food containers for the children to pack for their travels. If the children are camping in a wilderness area or spending a day at the beach, it is important for them to know that litter is not left on the ground. Each location has specific rules about garbage. Encourage children to share their travel experiences while playing in the center. Perhaps they have camped in a wilderness area and know about carrying their garbage out of protected areas, or maybe they have hiked on trails and have learned how it is important to stay on the trail to protect the plant life.

ACTIVITIES FOR CURRICULUM AREAS

READING & LANGUAGE DEVELOPMENT CENTER ACTIVITIES

· · · · · Caring for Earth Lotto Game · · · · ·

Materials Needed: patterns on page 107, scissors, construction paper, markers, glue

Directions: During this activity the children will be identifying many common things—some which are manufactured, others which are natural. Before preparing the materials decide how the children will complete the lotto game. If the children are matching pictures, make two photocopies of the pattern page. However, if the children are ready to match labeled pictures with words, provide a lotto board that only shows the words. To do this, cover the pictures before making a copy of the board. (Refer to pattern page 16 to see how the board should look.) For the playing cards make a copy of the pattern page with the pictures shown. When finished making the photocopies, mount them on construction paper and cut apart one photocopy to make the playing cards. Color the pictures as desired and set the materials in the center. After the children are familiar with the pictures shown on the playing cards, invite them to play the lotto game by matching the picture card in the corresponding space on the board. If appropriate, ask the children to place all pictures of items that are manufactured in one group and to talk about these items.

Variation: To give children opportunities to work with new vocabulary words, write the new words on a poster board, leaving extra space for the pictures that children clip from nature magazines. The pictures on the lotto board pattern page can be used to start the list.

· · · · · Thinking About Earth · · · · ·

Materials Needed: poem on page 108, tape recorder and headphones, watercolor marker, laminating material, craft stick, construction paper

Directions: This beautiful poem certainly encourages children to reflect on what they see in nature. Record the poem on cassette tape for the children. Decorate a craft stick to use as a pointer when following along with the recording. Enlarge the poem at 120% and photocopy it on 11" x 17" (279 x 432 mm) copier paper. Mount the copy on construction paper and laminate it. In the center invite the child to "read" the words of the poem while listening to the recording. If it is appropriate, indicate which letters you would like the child to circle with a watercolor marker.

····· Our Beautiful Oceans and Rain Forests ·····

Materials Needed: books about the rain forest and ocean, magazine pictures, small cassette player with headphones, nature music tapes (ocean sounds, rain forest sounds), construction paper, crayons

Directions: As you gather materials for the center, you may wish to consider purchasing small walkman cassette players with headphones since they are affordable and work well in centers. This activity offers an excellent opportunity for the children to "read" books or study pictures about oceans and rain forests with a partner. (Be sure to include some pictures of coral reefs and kelp forests.) Invite the children to look at rain forest pictures or ocean pictures while listening to the nature tapes. Some children may be excited about drawing their own pictures of the ocean and rain forest while listening to the nature music. Perhaps the pictures could be displayed in the center.

····· Who Litters? Not Me! Puppet Show ·····

Materials Needed: animal puppets, brown lunch bags, craft items, watercolor markers, paste or glue, construction paper scraps, scissors, books about recycling, pictures of pollution

Directions: Who litters? Where should we put the trash? Children can explore these questions when giving a puppet show. First, gather materials for making puppets or provide commercial animal puppets. If the children are making their puppets, they might be interested in using natural objects (pinecones, pine needles, leaves) and recyclable items (plastic caps, soda can tabs, newspapers) to decorate their puppets. Encourage the children to create a show with their new puppets to tell others about caring for the earth by recycling materials and by not littering.

····· Telling "Earthwise" Stories ·····

Materials Needed: patterns on pages 109–110, scissors, construction paper, glue

Directions: These pictures can tell a story! Invite the children to think about how these people are helping us keep the earth clean. To prepare the picture cards, photocopy the pattern pages. *Note:* You may wish to enlarge the pictures before making the copies. Mount the pictures on construction paper and then cut them apart. Encourage the child to talk about the pictures with a partner and then think of a story that incorporates some of the pictures.

Variation: Sort the pictures into sets and have the children arrange them in sequential order.

Caring for Earth

clouds	rain	smoke and fire
sun	water	trees
paper	aluminum cans	glass bottles
animals	flowers	plastic bottles

Quiet Feelings

When quiet feelings come to me,

I sit as still as still can be.

I think about trees or a pretty tune,

Or storybook time, or a big, full moon.

I think about darkness covering the town,

Or twinkling stars as I'm lying down.

I think about wings on a butterfly,

Or clouds moving gently across the sky.

I think about leaves, or a nest in the tree,

And all of these bring quiet feelings to me.

–*Louise Binder Scott*

WRITING CENTER ACTIVITIES

· · · · · My Favorite Place in Nature · · · · ·

Materials Needed: nature magazines, newspapers, decorative rubber stamps, stamp pad, construction paper, scissors, paste, colored pencils

Directions: What is your favorite scenic spot? Do you enjoy viewing the mountains? the ocean? a quiet lake? Encourage each child to look at pictures of nature scenes in magazines and choose a favorite. To finish the project, have the child cut out the favorite picture and paste it on construction paper. Of course the picture must have a delightful frame; so encourage the child to print small images around the outer edges of the paper by using rubber stamps. Have the child cut out letters from newspapers to make a title for his picture or "write" the title with colored pencils. If there is space on the paper, encourage him to write about why he likes this special place.

· · · · · I Can Help! Booklet · · · · ·

Materials Needed: patterns on pages 113–114, construction paper, stapler, pencil, magazines, scissors, paste, scraps of recyclable items, masking tape

Directions: Some children may enjoy making booklets about recycling, especially ones which emphasize how children can help. Duplicate one copy of the booklet cover and four or five copies of the booklet page for each child. Now the child must think about things which can be recycled as well as other things which cannot be recycled. Have the child cut out pictures and glue them on the booklet pages. She must then complete the sentences by naming the objects. Perhaps you would like the children to work with scraps of actual materials by taping them in the booklets (if those items are recycled in your neighborhood)—for example, newspaper, sections from plastic bags that show the recycling symbol, pieces from clean milk jug, soda can tabs, pieces of junk mail, pages from an old telephone book, shiny magazine covers, etc. When the booklet pages are finished, assemble the pages and staple them together along the left edge of the cover. Now the booklet is ready for the child to proudly "read" to family members or friends.

· · · · · Rain Forest Crunch · · · · ·

Materials Needed: shredded coconut, chocolate chips, chopped nuts, cupcake liners, spoons, crayons, paper, patterns on page 115, scissors, glue, construction paper, actual package of rain forest crunch

Directions: Gather the necessary items for making the rain forest crunch and place them in small plastic containers. *Note:* Before serving the snack, be sure the children are **not** allergic to nuts. Photocopy the instruction cards and cut them apart. Mount the cards on construction paper. In the center, have the children follow the instructions on the cards to prepare their snacks. When the children have finished eating the snack, encourage them to draw a picture of what they ate and to write words that describe how the snack tasted.

· · · · · Stampin' Out Garbage · · · · ·

Materials Needed: alphabet rubber stamps, stamp pad, plastic lowercase letters, tempera paint, paper towels, paper (construction paper, newsprint or brown paper bags)

Directions: Young printers will be busy in this center stampin' out garbage (words about recycling, cleaning up our community, preventing pollution and so on). If you prefer to prepare some printed words for the children to copy, display those in the center. *Note:* Some children may wish to know how to spell certain words, others will use invented spelling. If the children are using plastic letters to stamp a message, dampen a paper towel on a Styrofoam tray with tempera paint to make a "paint" pad. Demonstrate how to press the letter into the paint and then make a print on the paper. To help the children understand about reusing different materials, provide brown grocery bags that are cut into sections to use when making prints.

· · · · · Cooperative Environmental Posters · · · · ·

Materials Needed: large construction paper sheets or paper grocery bags, markers, nature magazines, colored pencils, pencils, scissors, paste, scissors that cut decorative edges, environmental posters

Directions: Even young learners can think about messages for others to read on posters. To prepare the materials, cut the grocery bags into large flat pieces or provide construction paper for the children to use when making their posters. Have the children work with partners as they create the posters with the provided materials. Explain how important it is for them to use peace-keeping skills by working together, sharing materials and communicating their ideas. These interpersonal skills also apply to taking care of our earth through cooperative efforts.

I Can Help!

I cannot recycle

I can recycle

Take a paper cup
and spoon.

Place I spoonful of
coconut in cup.

Add I spoonful of nuts.

Add I spoonful of
chocolate drops.

Mix together.

Eat and enjoy.

MATH CENTER ACTIVITIES

· · · · · Cash in the Trash · · · · ·

Materials Needed: picture card patterns on page 118, 40 pennies (play money or actual coins), poster board, marker, construction paper

Directions: There actually is cash in the trash if we do not recycle aluminum cans. This is one resource that is 100% recyclable. To play this game, provide four copies of the picture cards that are cut apart and mounted on construction paper. Invite the children to play with partners and "collect" aluminum cans. To begin play, stack the cards in a pile and turn them *face down*. Each child draws a card and collects the corresponding number of pennies—one penny per can. The game ends when each player has collected 20 pennies. Remember that each player must collect no more than 20 pennies. If the last card drawn shows too many cans, place the card on the discard pile and draw another card.

· · · · · Collect and Count · · · · ·

Materials Needed: milk jug caps (different colors), soda bottle caps, 10 clean plastic frosting containers or margarine containers with lids, permanent marker, patterns on pages 119–120, construction paper

Directions: Ask parents to collect milk jug caps, frosting or margarine containers and soda bottle caps for this center activity. When you have enough materials, decide if the children will work with numbers from 6 to 15 or 11 to 20. Using a permanent marker write a predetermined numeral on each plastic container. For the activity, encourage pairs of children to count and fill each plastic container with the corresponding number of caps. When they are finished with the task, direct the children to select a mat and place a numbered container on each star. Now the children must think about those numbers and then place another numbered container on a left or right circle. (This container shows a quantity that is more or less than the numbered container that is covering the star.) Continue the process until both mats have four containers on them. Of course this activity can be repeated several times by placing different containers on the circles having stars.

Variation: If identical plastic containers or juice cans were filled with soda can tabs, milk jug caps and soda bottle caps, would they weigh the same? Children can investigate this question by weighing the containers on a bucket balance. Encourage the children to explore the different weights of the containers when they hold the same number of each item or when they are filled to capacity. Be sure to ask the children to predict which container is heavier or lighter before they weigh them. Also, when the containers are filled to capacity with items, invite the children to empty the containers and compare the quantities by predicting which pile of caps or tabs are fewer in number. Then have the children count the items.

· · · · · Tubes 'n' Measurements · · · · ·

Materials Needed: toilet paper tubes, wrapping paper tubes, paper towel tubes, index cards, pencil, paint

Directions: Long tubes. Short tubes. How many tubes is the distance from a desk to the door? If more than a third of our garbage is paper, then why not rescue paper tubes from the trash and reuse them in the classroom? Paint the tubes with bright primary colors to make them colorful. The children can use different sizes of paper tubes for measuring objects. Another option is to plan a "Measure Treasure Hunt" and give the children clues about selected objects in the room. Simple questions along with diagrams can be written on index cards for the children to use. For example: Find two objects that are 2 tubes in length. Find an object that is longer than one wrapping paper tube or two wrapping paper tubes. The possibilities are endless!

· · · · · Pickin' and Packin' Cartons · · · · ·

Materials Needed: different-sized paper milk cartons (pint, quart, half gallon), cardboard box

Directions: Here is an activity that encourages children to investigate different ways to fill the box. To prepare for the activity, find a cardboard box that holds several large paper milk cartons and several of each size of paper milk cartons. Clean the cartons with soapy water and allow them to dry. Close each carton and staple it. In the center encourage the children to figure out what is the fewest number of cartons that can fit in the box and what is the greatest number of cartons.

· · · · · Patterns of Caps · · · · ·

Materials Needed: milk jug caps (10 caps in four different colors), two egg cartons, scissors

Directions: Patterning with milk jug caps—it is possible. To prepare the materials, cut off the lid on each egg carton and staple the two cartons together to make two rows of 12 cavities. Start the patterns for the children to finish by placing a milk jug cap in the first four cavities of each row. You can create ABAB, AABB or AABAAB patterns for the children to complete. Have the child drop additional milk jug caps in the egg cartons to finish the repeat patterns.

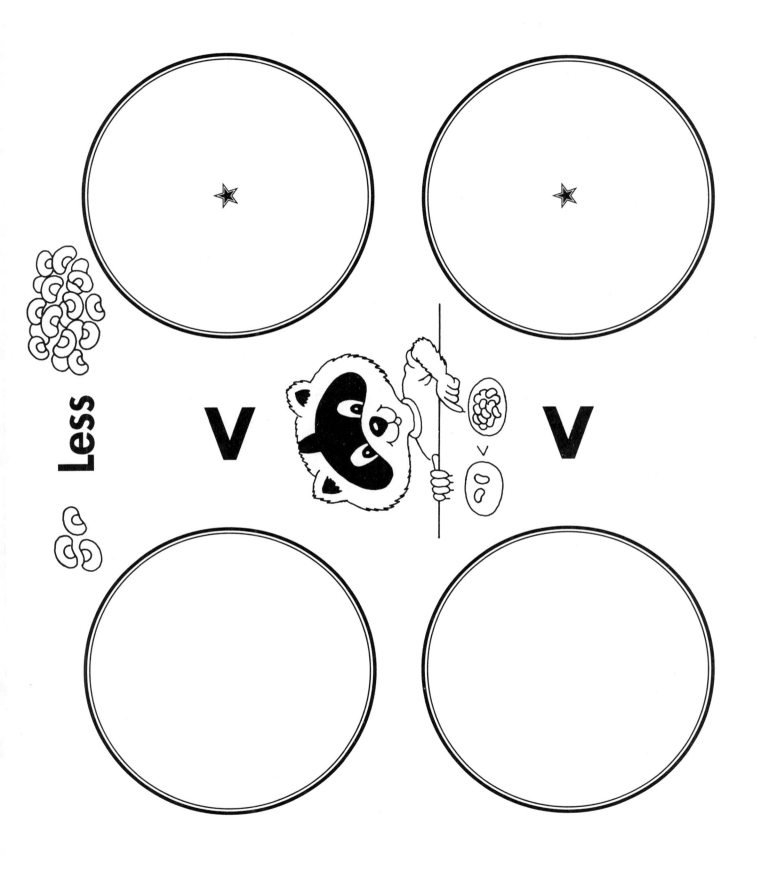

Less

V

V

119

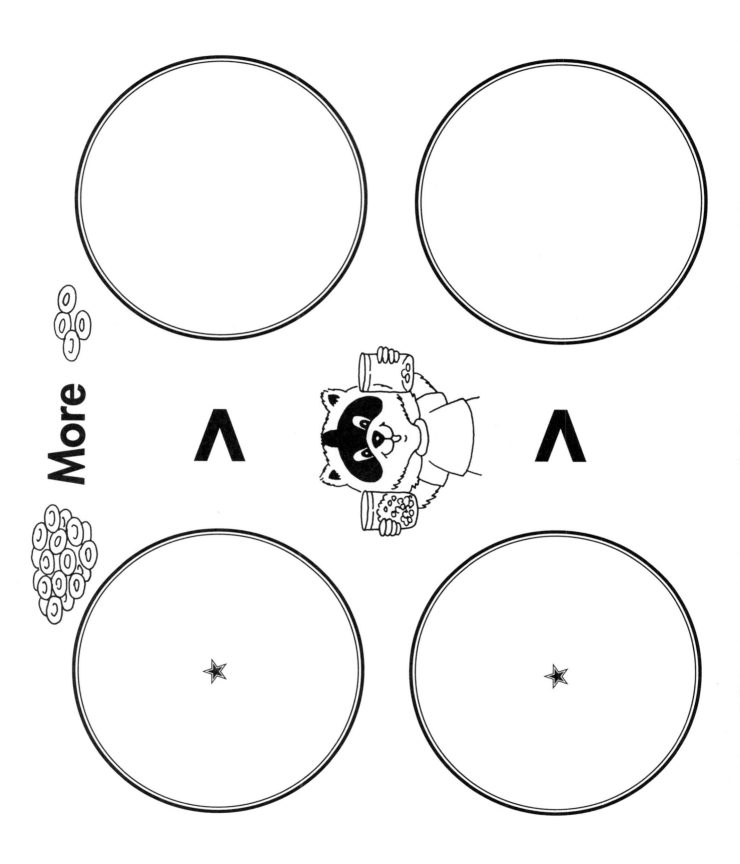

More

SCIENCE CENTER ACTIVITIES

· · · · · Separate, Sort and Recycle · · · · ·

Materials Needed: clean aluminum and plastic containers, newspaper, metal tin cans, magnet, brown paper grocery bags, items that cannot be recycled, marker, small plastic storage bin (if possible, made from recycled plastic), books on recycling, magnets

Directions: Children can separate and sort recyclable materials by placing them in corresponding paper bags that have been labeled—metals, paper (newspaper), plastic. It may be helpful to tape a sample of the corresponding material on the paper bag. *Note:* You may wish to find out which materials are being recycled in your community. If different kinds of paper (newspaper, copier paper, glossy magazines, junk mail, telephone books) are being collected in separate containers in your community, the children may be interested in separating these types of paper. Another natural investigation for children is to test metal containers with a magnet and then separate the metals into two groups. It is almost magical to watch how magnets are attracted to tin and steel but not aluminum. For this center activity the children may also "read" books about recycling.

· · · · · Nature's Carpet Cleaners · · · · ·

Materials Needed: earthworms, large clear plastic storage containers or ice cream pails with lids, soil (humus), ground dwelling insects (ants and beetles), tiny pieces of food scraps, magnifying glass, two soil samples, small clear plastic jars (peanut butter jars), water, craft sticks or tongue depressors, soup spoon

Directions: Collect some garden soil that has plenty of compost or humus material (bits of grass clipping, leaves or other decaying plant material) in it from a gardener. The compost material helps retain moisture in the soil as well as providing added nutrients for the plants. Place the soil along with earthworms and small beetles in a large clear plastic storage container that has a cover. Also collect some soil that contains mostly sand or clay particles and a slight amount of humus material. Encourage the children to investigate what earthworms and beetles eat and how they are needed by plants.

Have the children compare the two soil samples by observing them through magnifying glasses and also by testing them. To test the soil, have the children place several spoonfuls of each soil in a plastic jar. Add water to fill the jars over half full. Secure the lid on each jar and then shake them. Watch how the different materials in the soil separate and settle to the bottom of the jar. It may take more than 30 minutes for the water to clear.

· · · · · Mixed-Up with Oil and Water · · · · ·

Materials Needed: vegetable oil, medicine cups, water, food coloring, toothpicks, paper towels, pictures of oil spills and animals coated with oil, clean dropper bottle, waxed paper, trays

Directions: What happens when oil is spilled on a body of water? (During group time show pictures of oil spills and the devastation that occurs.) Young children can investigate how oil and water do not mix. For this activity, fill a medicine cup half full with oil. Have the child add two different colors of food coloring (only **one** drop of each color) and observe the results. Encourage the child to move the drops of food coloring with a toothpick and then add **two or three** drops of water to the oil. Invite the child to move the water drop in the oil with the toothpick. The child will discover that the food coloring droplets will combine with the water but not the oil. Encourage the child to stir the oil and notice how the water drop breaks into droplets but later the droplets combine into one. When finished investigating, ask the child to talk about her observations and what happens when a large amount of oil is spilled on a pond, lake or ocean. To help the children understand how oil floats on water, have them fill medicine cups with water and enough oil to be visible. Children can also investigate how oil does not disappear or evaporate like water. To do this, have the child place several drops of oil and water on a piece of paper toweling, label the towel and allow it to dry on the waxed paper. At a later time, discuss the observations.

· · · · · Our Interesting Earth · · · · ·

Materials Needed: water, rocks, bark, bugs, potting soil, seeds, fossils, shells, sand (roadside, ocean beach), soil from woodland, various soil samples, twigs, tree branch cut into miniature logs (observe tree rings), magnifying lenses, clean Styrofoam trays, moss, lichens, bucket balance

Directions: Here is a perfect opportunity to let children closely study natural items. Place the gathered materials on Styrofoam trays or in resealable plastic bags. For the activity, encourage the children to compare and contrast the materials. For example, observe how sand is actually tiny pieces of rocks. Provide a bucket balance and encourage the children to compare the weights of samples.

· · · · · Plant a Seed, Grow a Tree · · · · ·

Materials Needed: tree seedlings, water in bucket, soil, books about trees, tree seeds, planting containers, magnifying lenses, water, water sprayer

Directions: For this activity children can "adopt" trees and learn about caring for them. Provide materials for the children to use for planting tree seeds in small potting containers. Use a water sprayer to moisten the soil. Invite the child to examine the larger tree seedlings to find out about the parts of a tree. When the children are finished examining the seedlings, plant the trees as a class project.

ART CENTER ACTIVITIES

· · · · · Earth Creations · · · · ·

Materials Needed: tempera paint (blue, brown and green), paintbrushes, large paper, painting smocks, world map, easel

Directions: Here is an opportunity for young children to think about how the earth has land and water. Display the world map in the art center. Encourage the child to study the map, identifying land masses and bodies of water (oceans). After studying the map, perhaps the child is inspired to paint her own version of the world. Allow the paintings to dry before displaying them on the walls.

· · · · · Land Formations in Clay · · · · ·

Materials Needed: brown, green and blue project clay (recipe on page 30), globe, craft sticks, toothpicks, plastic knives, pictures of land formations

Directions: For this activity, prepare project clay by following the recipe. During group time show pictures of land formations and encourage the children to share about what they have seen. If the child has traveled across plains or over hills or mountains, encourage the child to show what the land looks like by making a clay model. Some children may not have had these experiences. It is important for them to see pictures before creating models in clay. As the children work on their models in the center be sure to encourage them to use "tools" to create different textures in the clay.

· · · · · Recyclable Creations · · · · ·

Materials Needed: plastic, paper and metal recyclables, masking tape, electrical tape, index cards, pencils

Directions: What can be made out of recyclable items? Use your imagination and soon you will have an idea to recreate something from trash. To collect materials for this project ask parents to donate recyclable goods. Store the collected materials in a labeled bin. As the children build their dimensional projects, let them tape the objects together with masking or electrical tape. When the projects are finished, have the children name their creations and display the names on index cards.

· · · · · Printing Trash · · · · ·

Materials Needed: lids, caps, soda cans, crumpled newspaper, crumpled plastic bags, soda can tabs, tempera paints, paper towels, Styrofoam trays, newsprint

Directions: Search for interesting shapes of recyclable materials for young artists to use when printing. The children can create delightful prints with the materials by dipping them in tempera paint and then lightly pressing the paint-covered objects on the newsprint. Encourage the children to continue until they have created delightful designs on the papers. Be sure to use several colors while printing. For a printing pad, just pour some tempera paint on a paper towel that rests on a Styrofoam tray.

Variation: Print on large brown paper bags instead of newsprint. Obtain stationery and other items that are made out of recycled paper for the children to examine. The children can print their own stationery by using pieces of newsprint that have been cut into identical sheets of paper.

· · · · · It's My World Collages · · · · ·

Materials Needed: paper, crayons, markers, magazines, paste, newspaper, scissors, pencils, natural objects (optional)

Directions: Our beautiful world can be enjoyed by everyone. Have the children think about the Earth and what is important to them. For the activity, encourage each child to collect pictures, and natural objects which are glued on paper. When finished, let him "write" words to express what is felt about the Earth.

Variation: Perhaps the children may be interested in including rubbings of natural objects along with glued-on items when making their collages.

I AM SPECIAL

Building children's self-esteem is a very important role for teachers and parents. Letting children know that they are special and helping them realize how much they can accomplish independently are two ways to help them feel confident. During the school year, the children will have opportunities to make new friends, learn how to be sensitive to others and become good listeners. These socialization skills are also an important part of the child's emotional development. Finally, by giving children respect and encouragement, they know their contributions are valued.

Change your classroom into a learning environment that highlights the work of your young learners. If possible, display pictures of the children involved with classroom activities along with pictures of them with their friends and family members. Also include posters of other children playing, investigating and interacting with children of different ethnicity. A special classroom banner can be made that features each child's picture along with a handprint. Under each picture include the child's name.

In addition to the center activities that are offered in this theme, gather other materials for instant centers: tabletop and floor puzzles, related flannel board materials, picture card sets, nutrition materials, parts of the body materials, using our senses materials, and so on. As you set up your centers, be sure to include books about friendships, families, children of different ethnic groups, feelings and emotions, children having physical or mental impairments, our bodies and how we use the five senses, and occupations for the children to "read" in your library corner. During group time talk about why the children are special. Be sure to emphasize the pleasures that all children share to help them accept other children who are physically or mentally challenged. If available, share informative picture books that are wonderful discussion starters.

· · · · · The Dramatic Play Center · · · · ·

This center is the perfect location for "celebrating" birthdays or for children to interact in a "home" setting. If it is a party celebration, provide shaving cream, cake pan, food coloring, glitter, and of course, candles. Let the child create a colorful cake batter and top it with candles. Another suggestion is to transform the center into a family room setting by offering play food, utensils, pictures, telephone, and a few pieces of furniture for the children to use. The possibilities are endless for role playing.

ACTIVITIES FOR CURRICULUM AREAS

READING & LANGUAGE DEVELOPMENT CENTER ACTIVITIES

· · · · · I Can Rhyme Puzzles · · · · ·

Materials Needed: picture puzzle patterns on pages 129–130, construction paper, scissors, envelope for pieces, watercolor markers

Directions: Sort, match and rhyme! What a delightful way to think about pictures/words while assembling small puzzles. To prepare the four miniature puzzles, photocopy the pattern pages and mount them on construction paper. Color the pictures with markers. To ensure that young learners can easily sort the puzzle pieces, use a marker to give each puzzle a different colored frame. Finish the set of puzzles by cutting apart the pictures on the dashed lines. Be sure to make one vertical cut line through the picture and the word (separating the initial consonant from the remaining portion of the word). In the center, the children may assemble the puzzles and talk about the initial consonant sounds and rhyming words. When the rhyming words are identified, have the child place the matching pairs together.

· · · · · A Friendship Train · · · · ·

Materials Needed: large size index cards, marker, photographs of children, scissors, glue, plastic capital letters, large poster board that shows all of the children and their first names

Directions: Let's make a train! To make this delightful game, obtain individual photographs of the children and yourself and then photocopy each picture. Using a marker draw a vertical line through the middle of the cards. Glue your picture on the left side of one card and a student's picture on the right side. To make more cards for the train, glue pictures of your students on the other cards. Write a number below each picture so the children can arrange the cards in numerical order. If you have more than 20 children in the classroom, you may wish to make two shorter trains. This way the children can work with numbers that are smaller than 20. Of course, this is also an excellent opportunity for the children to think about initial consonant and vowel sounds by placing the corresponding plastic letter below each child's picture. If it is possible, provide a chart that shows all the children and their first names so that those young learners who need assistance can look at the chart.

Variation: Another idea is to make a Friendship Train puzzle for the children to assemble. To make puzzle cuts, overlap the cards and cut through both thicknesses by making a zigzag or wavy edge. Continue until all cards have edges that interlock when placed side by side.

····· I Can Do It! ·····

Materials Needed: picture card patterns on pages 131–132, construction paper, scissors, envelope for picture cards, watercolor markers, items to match (toothbrush, shoelace, comb, zipper, small shirt that has buttons, washcloth, bar of soap, markers, small book, dotted lines on paper for printing name, pencil, plastic fork, empty shampoo bottle)

Directions: Can you can tie a shoe? wash your face? brush your teeth? Young learners will have to think about 12 different tasks that they can complete independently or with only a little assistance. Here's a wonderful way to emphasize their accomplishments. Just collect the necessary items that will be matched with the picture cards. Photocopy the picture patterns and mount them on construction paper. Cut apart the cards and color them with markers. Place the cards along with the actual items in a container. In the center, the child may draw one picture card at a time and match it with an object that goes with it. Encourage him to set the item on the corresponding card. When the child is finished with the task, talk about what he is able to do without assistance.

····· Express Your Feelings ·····

Materials Needed: picture card patterns on page 133, construction paper, scissors, envelope for picture cards, watercolor markers, books about feelings, unbreakable mirror, pencil

Directions: For this activity children surely will delight in making faces while looking at themselves in a mirror. Photocopy the patterns and mount them on construction paper. Cut apart the picture cards. Invite the child to look at each picture and change her facial expression to convey the same feeling. She may also match the picture cards with the word cards by comparing the words. Encourage her to read the picture cards to a partner. Provide some blank cards for the children to use. Have each child draw a facial expression and then make the same expression while looking at a mirror. Encourage the child to talk about this facial expression with her partner.

····· "W" for Wiggles ·····

Materials Needed: tape recorder and headphones, poem on page 134, large unbreakable mirror, two watercolor markers, laminating material

Directions: Of course children love to wiggle, so here is the perfect opportunity for them to shake, wiggle and giggle. To prepare for this activity, locate a large unbreakable full-length mirror for the children to use as they observe how they move their bodies. Photocopy the poem, mount it on construction paper and laminate it. Before placing the materials in the center record the poem. In the center, let the children listen to the poem and moving their bodies accordingly. At the end of the recording instruct the child to circle all "Ww"s in the poem. Indicate which colored marker the child should use and any other letters that should be circled.

block

clock

ball

wall

comb my hair

shampoo my hair

brush my teeth

tie my shoe

feed myself

wash my hands

read a book

draw a picture

button my shirt

zip my jacket

wash my face

print my name

happy	happy	sad
sad	angry	angry
tired	tired	

Wiggles

A wiggle wiggle here,

A wiggle wiggle there,

Wiggle your hands up in the air.

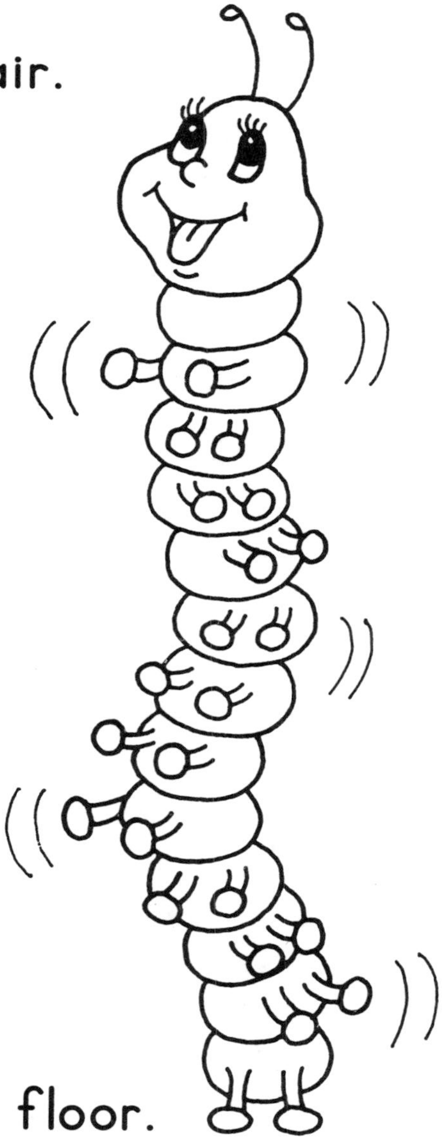

Wiggle your shoulders,

Wiggle your hips,

Wiggle your knees,

And move your lips.

Wiggle, wiggle, wiggle,

And wiggle some more;

And now let's sit down on the floor.

–Adapted from Louise Binder Scott

WRITING CENTER ACTIVITIES

· · · · · All About Me Books · · · · ·

Materials Needed: booklet page pattern on page 137, paste, photographs of children and families, pencils, construction paper, paper, magazines, scissors

Directions: It is always special to make a book about yourself! Here is an opportunity for each child to make and keep a personal book. Ask parents to send pictures of their families for their children to use in the booklet. Photocopy these pictures of families. If you have not taken individual pictures of the students, you will also need to have individual photographs for the booklets. To prepare the activity materials, photocopy the pictures of families and individual children. Assemble a booklet for each child by folding a sheet of construction paper in half for the booklet cover. Include a folded copy of the booklet page. Staple the booklet along the left side of the cover. Use a marker to write the booklet title "All About Me" on the cover. In the writing center, invite the child to paste his pictures in the booklet and complete the sentences. The back of the second page can be used as the third page of the booklet by encouraging the child to find a picture of something he likes or a place he likes to visit. Have the child "write" a sentence about that picture.

· · · · · Friendly Adventures · · · · ·

Materials Needed: chart paper, watercolor markers, pictures of children, scissors, paste

Directions: During group time write a story about an imaginary trip. Involve the children in the story by using their names for the characters. Record the story on chart paper and paste photocopies of the children's pictures above their names. (You may wish to write several short stories during the month. This way all of the children's names will be used.) Draw simple objects near selected nouns to help the children remember the story. Place the story in the center for the children to "read" and blank chart paper for children to write their own stories. Be sure to supply additional photocopies of the children's pictures for your young budding authors to use.

· · · · · Card Fun · · · · ·

Materials Needed: paper, markers, rubber stamps, stamp pads, crayons, scraps of tissue paper, craft materials, glitter, glue, colored pencils, scissors

Directions: Some children will need no encouragement to make cards for friends and family members. Be sure to gather enough interesting materials with which to decorate the cards. Of course, have the children include special messages in their beautiful cards.

· · · · · Music and Feelings · · · · ·

Materials Needed: paper, music cassettes, tape player with headphones, paper, pencils

Directions: Music certainly can convey emotions and feelings. Encourage the children to listen to different kinds of music and then "write," draw pictures or use scribble writing to convey their thoughts about the music and how it makes them feel.

· · · · · A Booklet About My Kindergarten Friends · · · · ·

Materials Needed: pattern on page 140, pencils, pictures of the children, glue, construction paper, stapler, scissors

Directions: This classroom booklet will be a favorite for the children. To make this special booklet, photocopy the completed picture frame that is used in the activity Friendship Math and mount it on construction paper. (This will be exciting for students to see their pictures on the cover.) Decide with the children during group time what they would like to tell about themselves in the booklet. Take this information and make a booklet page that each child can complete. In the center, have each child finish the booklet page and then glue a photocopy of her/his picture on it. When all of the pages are complete, assemble them into a booklet. Staple the pages and booklet cover together to bind the book. Your class book is now complete. The children will surely enjoy "reading" this book with family members.

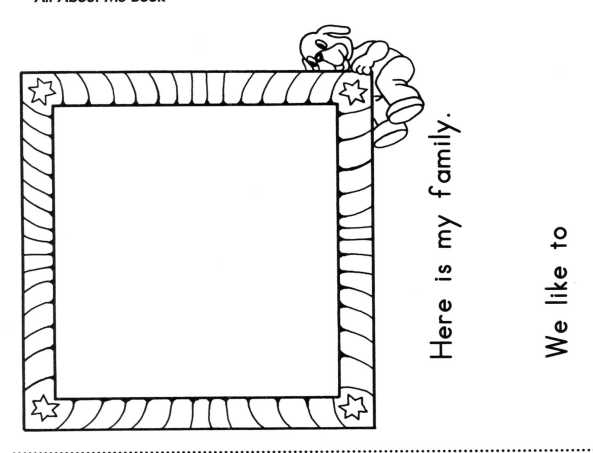

Here is my family.

We like to

My name is

I like to

MATH CENTER ACTIVITIES

· · · · · Measuring My Growth · · · · ·

Materials Needed: links or linking cubes, pencil, string wrapped on craft stick

Directions: Here is an interesting way to involve children with nonstandard units of measurement. Have the children work with partners and measure their heights with links or linking cubes. To do this, one child should lie down on the floor while the other child makes a chain to match the child's length. Repeat the process for the partner's length. When the children are finished they can compare their chains to determine which person is shorter or taller.

· · · · · I Can Sort! · · · · ·

Materials Needed: plastic numerals, plastic letters, plastic shapes

Directions: Some children may need to practice sorting letters and numbers. Here is an opportunity for them to sort a variety of pieces into three categories.

Variation: If the plastic numerals, letters and shapes are available in different colors, encourage the children to sort all of the pieces by color rather than by shape. Pose this as a problem and encourage them to figure out how they can sort all of the pieces in a different way.

· · · · · Patterning with Handprints and Footprints · · · · ·

Materials Needed: tagboard (two different colors), scissors, pencil

Directions: Here is a delightful repeat patterning activity. To make the materials, cut out enough handprints and footprints from tagboard for the children to use. The children can make ABAB, ABBA or AABB patterns with the cutouts. The pattern pieces may differ in shape or color. Just help the children get started by placing the first three or four shapes of the pattern on a tabletop or floor.

Variations: The children may be interested in making their own handprints or footprints and using them to measure objects in the room. Challenge the children by creating problems that may have different solutions. For example, find objects that are smaller (larger) than your handprint or 2 handprints in length.

· · · · · So Many Friendly Faces · · · · ·

Materials Needed: children's pictures, frame pattern on page 140, construction paper, scissors, glue, counters, plastic numerals

Directions: Take pictures of the children in different sized groups to show sets from 2–8. For example, the first picture shows two children, the second picture shows three children (1 + 2), the third picture shows four children (2+2), the fourth picture shows five children (3 + 2), the fifth picture shows six children (3 + 3), the sixth picture shows seven children (4 + 3) and the seventh picture shows eight children (4 + 4). Make two or three photocopies of each print and mount them on construction paper. To complete the pattern on page 140 make a photocopy of the page and then fill each box with a child's individual photograph which is also used in the "All About Me" booklets. When the pattern page is complete, make another photocopy of the page and laminate it to preserve it.

This activity will surely please the young mathematicians. The children can work with the materials several different ways. They can sort the picture cards by matching the same sets with a corresponding plastic numeral. Another suggestion is they can arrange one copy of each set in sequential order from smallest to largest (or vice versa). Some children will enjoy the challenge of working with numbers greater than 10 by counting the friends in the big frame. Have the young learner cover each individual photograph with a math counter as she counts the faces to find out how many are shown in the picture frame. She can use the "Counting Chart" on page 47 to record her results.

· · · · · It's Family Math · · · · ·

Materials Needed: photographs of families, lima beans or other math counters, construction paper, glue, scissors, poster board, marker

Directions: Counting members of several families is certainly a different way to strengthen math skills. To prepare for this activity, use the pictures of the children's families that are collected for the booklets "All About Me." Make a photocopy of each picture and mount them on construction paper. Determine how many people are in the smallest-size families and the largest-size families. On poster board write down the smallest number at the top of the chart and the largest number at the bottom. Fill in with the remaining numbers to complete the sequence. For this activity encourage the child to work with a partner and sort the pictures according to the number of people in each family. If it is appropriate, the child may wish to cover the people with counters as he counts them. When the pictures are sorted, the children may graph the results on the chart by placing all of the pictures of families having three people after the number 3 and so on. Discuss the results with the children by asking them to determine which family size is the most common for the classroom.

Friendship Math Pattern

SCIENCE CENTER ACTIVITIES

· · · · · What's Missing? · · · · ·

Materials Needed: pattern on page 143, scissors, construction paper, glue, unbreakable mirror

Directions: For this activity children will learn to identify parts of the face and head. If the children need a lot of practice naming these body parts, have them work with partners as they name and locate the parts of the face and head. To prepare the materials, duplicate two copies of the pattern page and mount them on construction paper. Cut apart the pictures of one copy to make the playing cards. In the center, encourage the child to find matching pairs by placing the playing card on the lotto board. When finished, have the child tell a partner what is missing in each picture. Be sure the child uses the correct term to explain her reasoning.

· · · · · Family Foods · · · · ·

Materials Needed: picture card patterns on page 144, magazines, construction paper, scissors, crayons, paste

Directions: Everyone has favorite foods, even young learners. This activity gives your students an opportunity to clip pictures of foods their families enjoy eating. Reproduce a copy of the food picture cards for each child. To begin the activity, encourage each child to cut apart the labeled picture cards and glue them on construction paper. Invite the children to clip pictures of foods from magazines. They can identify those foods by drawing a line from the corresponding picture card to the magazine picture. Of course, if they find pictures of their favorite foods, those pictures are glued near the "yum-yum" card. When the children are finished with the activity, have them share about foods their families enjoy eating.

· · · · · Using My Senses Game · · · · ·

Materials Needed: picture card patterns on page 144, five common objects (things to see, smell, touch, and/or hear), two or three special foods to taste in sealed containers, brown grocery bag, egg carton

Directions: For this game think about objects that can be seen, heard, smelled, or touched. Reproduce the picture cards for the senses and make 10 copies for the children to use. Mount the pictures on construction paper and then cut apart the pictures. Store them in an egg carton. Be sure to remove the cards that show an animal tasting food. Place the gathered items in a paper bag and set all of the materials in a labeled bin. To play the game have the child work with a partner and take turns picking something from the bag. Encourage the children to decide if they can see the object, touch the object, hear a noise, or smell an odor. If the child can observe an object by using four senses, have her place the "Wow" card near it. (*Note:* Be sure to explain to them that they should not taste anything unless an adult says it is safe to eat.) As each object is discussed, have the children place the corresponding picture cards near the object. When the children are finished with these objects, allow them to continue the investigation with special foods. (Obviously the children can see the foods and touch them before tasting them but cannot hear any noise when the foods are shaken in their hands.) When the children are finished making their observations, have them place the corresponding picture cards near each food.

· · · · · **Head, Shoulders, Knees, and Toes** · · · · ·

Materials Needed: patterns on pages 145–146, large unbreakable mirror, scissors, construction paper, glue

Directions: Our bodies are remarkable! Young children need time to observe how they are able to bend different parts of their bodies. This also is an opportunity for them to learn the names of those body parts. To prepare the materials, make two photocopies of the picture lotto board on page 145. Mount the copies on construction paper and cut apart one set of the pictures. If you prefer to have the children match words instead of pictures, cover the pictures on one of the copies and make a new photocopy that can be the lotto board. In the center the children can complete the lotto game. When the game is completed, let the child work with a partner and practice naming and locating the parts of her body that correspond with the picture cards. Another way to use the materials is to give the children the picture cards and an enlarged copy of the balloon toss scene (pattern page 146) which is mounted on poster board. Have the children look at the scene and match the corresponding picture cards near the arrows.

Variation: Perhaps you would like to record the traditional action rhyme, "Head, Shoulders, Knees, and Toes" for the children to follow while looking in a mirror.

· · · · · **Weather Feelings** · · · · ·

Materials Needed: weather flannel board set or teddy bear and clothing, flannel board, pictures of weather conditions

Directions: Locate clothing for a teddy bear or make cutouts of children and clothing from felt for a flannel board. Place the items in the center along with pictures of different weather conditions. The children may select a picture and then dress the bear or flannel board figures accordingly.

What's Missing?

fruits

vegetables

grains

dairy

proteins

Yum-yum!

see

smell

taste

hear

touch

Wow!

My Body

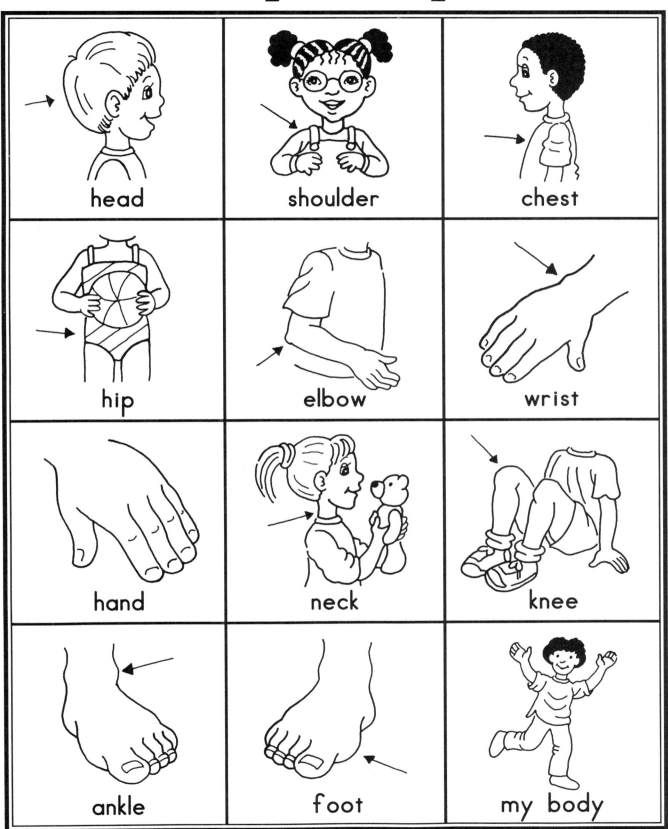

head

shoulder

chest

hip

elbow

wrist

hand

neck

knee

ankle

foot

my body

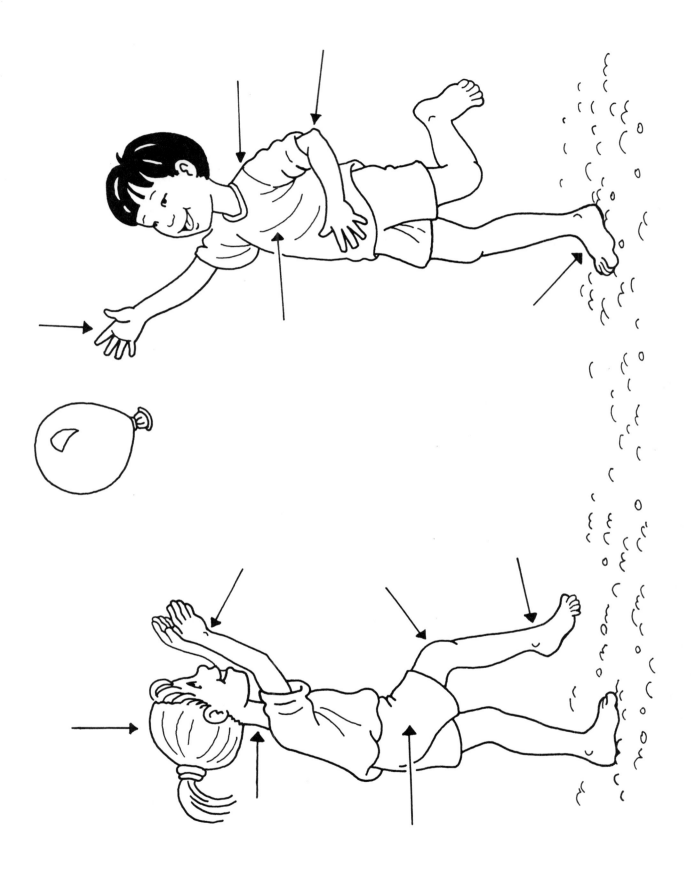

ART CENTER ACTIVITIES

····· Self-Portrait ·····

Materials Needed: unbreakable mirror, drawing paper, ethnic-colored crayons, crayons

Directions: Gather the necessary items and place them in a labeled container. Perhaps you would like to include your self-portrait for the children to see. Encourage them to look at themselves in the mirror and then draw their own portraits.

Materials Needed: large construction paper, crayons, ethnic-colored crayons, yarn, fabric scraps, scissors, craft materials

Directions: If the children would like to make paper doll shapes of their family members, cut out the shapes from construction paper. Let the children color and decorate the shapes with craft materials. They might like to add yarn for hair.

····· Friendship Beads ·····

Materials Needed: play clay or project clay (recipe on page 30), small paintbrush, elastic string or yarn

Directions: It is always fun to make beads from clay. Prepare the project clay by following the recipe or provide a different kind of play clay. Show the children how to form the clay into different shapes—spheres, cylinders, cubes, rectangular prisms. When the bead shapes are made, have each child use the handle end of a paintbrush to give each bead texture and also make a hole through the center of the shape. Allow the beads to dry before painting them and then stringing them as jewelry. The finished projects are perfect as gifts to share with friends and family members.

· · · · · A Favorite Collage · · · · ·

Materials Needed: magazines, construction paper, glue, fabric scraps, flat objects, scissors, favorite buttons, craft items

Directions: Here is an opportunity for children to express their interests. For these collages invite the children to find pictures of toys, foods, pets, animals, and other objects that they like. Have them glue the pictures on construction paper as well as favorite fabric scraps and craft items to make their collages look dimensional.

· · · · · My Favorite Color · · · · ·

Materials Needed: tempera paints, chart paper or bulletin board paper, tape, paintbrushes

Directions: This will be a large class project. On chart or bulletin board paper, the children can create a mural in wonderful vibrant colors. To prepare the materials, first "sign" the future mural by printing the names of the children in random order throughout the paper, leaving room for the young artists to paint pictures. Encourage the children to paint pictures using only their favorite colors. When the mural is finished, talk about how many children like red, blue, yellow, and so on.

· · · · · My Family, Pets and Feelings · · · · ·

Materials Needed: tempera paints, paper, easel, paintbrushes

Directions: Children will not need encouragement to paint pictures about families, pets and special interests. Just be sure there is an adequate supply of paper and paint! Their paintings can also be an expression about how they are feeling at the time.

IN THE GREEN, GREEN FOREST

Lush green forests not only offer beauty and a quiet escape from a hurried world for people, but also shelter for thousands of animals. Like the tropical rain forests the temperate deciduous forests are comprised of trees varying in height. The crowns of the tallest trees form a canopy that block most of the sunlight, keeping the forest floor cool and damp. Under this canopy live birds, squirrels and insects. Young trees thrive beneath this layer, forming the understory. Beneath the understory is a shrub layer that may be dense or sparse depending on the amount of sunlight that reaches this layer. When a mature tree dies, it still provides shelter for some animals. In the hollows of these dead trees live owls, opossums, or maybe raccoons. The leaf litter is home for numerous insects and other invertebrates, as well as chipmunks, moles, mice, salamanders, and reptiles. The plants, trees and animals vary according to the type of temperate forest (its climate and soil conditions). There are several kinds of temperate forests. The forest of oak and hickory trees is one familiar kind of forest. Within this forest are white oak trees that produce an abundance of acorns that support the lives of gray squirrels, chipmunks and other animals. Another kind of forest is the northern pine forest. Within this forest grow several kinds of pines, such as the eastern white pine. During the days of the pioneers, majestic white pine trees stood 200 feet tall with massive trunks 8 to 10 feet in diameter. In temperate rain forests of the Pacific Coast you can find giant trees such as the redwoods which are the world's tallest trees or the giant sequoia which are the largest in diameter.

Change your classroom into a forest environment by using the patterns for this theme. Using the opaque projector, trace the patterns on bulletin board paper and then paint them. As you set up your centers, be sure to include books about forests, trees and forest animals for the children to "read" in your library corner. During group time talk about forests or read aloud informative picture books. The following books are wonderful for sharing:

- Fisher, Ronald M. *A Day in the Woods.* National Geographic Society, 1975.
- Hirschi, Ron. *Who Lives in . . . the Forest?* Dodd, Mead & Company, 1987.
- Lavies, Bianca. *Tree Trunk Traffic.* E.P. Dutton, 1989.

· · · · · The Dramatic Play Center · · · · ·

Transform this center into a forest environment. Be imaginative as you adorn the space with decorations. Provide nature magazines, nature music, compass, canteens, stuffed animals (forest animals), sunglasses, ranger hats, hiking boots and vest, maps of parks, bird books, edible plant books, and other forest items. The children may decide to "hike" through the forest.

ACTIVITIES FOR CURRICULUM AREAS

READING & LANGUAGE DEVELOPMENT CENTER ACTIVITIES

· · · · · Life in the Forest Lotto · · · · ·

Materials Needed: pattern on page 153, construction paper, scissors, glue, markers

Directions: The fascinating world of a forest is right at your fingertips with this lotto set. By matching the pictures children learn to identify life in a forest as well as strengthen visual discrimination skills. To prepare the materials for this matching game, photocopy the pattern page two times and mount the copies on construction paper. Color as desired. Cut apart one set of picture cards as playing cards. The other copy of the pattern page will be the playing board. In the center have the child match the pictures and practice identifying the animals that are featured in this set.

Variation: You may prefer to show only the words on the lotto board. This is possible by covering the pictures on the pattern page and then making a photocopy. Mount your new board on construction paper and color it as desired. Perhaps the children need another visual discrimination task. Instead of using the materials as a lotto game, have the children sort and match identical pictures by providing three copies of each picture on the pattern page.

· · · · · Furry Chipmunks Finger Play · · · · ·

Materials Needed: tape recorder and headphones, finger play and pattern on page 154, watercolor markers, clear adhesive plastic, poster board, construction paper

Directions: Count backwards, listen for the "f" and "ch" sounds and think about chipmunks. These tasks keep young learners involved with this rhyme, which also is wonderful for group time as a finger play. To prepare for this activity, copy the poem on poster board. Be sure to leave plenty of space for the chipmunk cutouts. Cover the poster with clear adhesive plastic. At the end of the appropriate lines, attach Velcro buttons. Also attach Velcro to the backs of 10 chipmunks that have been photocopied and mounted on construction paper. Record the poem for the children to hear while "reading" the printed copy. At the end of the recording instruct the child to circle all "Ff" and "ch" letters in the poem. Indicate which colored markers the child should use. Now the materials are ready for the children to use. In the center have the child listen to the poem, attach the corresponding number of chipmunks and then circle the designated letters.

· · · · · Telling Forest Stories · · · · ·

Materials Needed: picture card patterns on page 155–156, scissors, glue, construction paper, markers, large envelope

Directions: What is the animal doing? What will the animal do next? For this activity, the child must look for visual clues, then sort and arrange the pictures in sequential order. To prepare the materials, reproduce the picture card patterns and color them as desired. Mount the copies on construction paper. Cut apart the pictures and store them in a large envelope. If you prefer to provide an answer key, number each series of cards with a different colored marker. Have the child sort the pictures and then place each set in sequential order. If appropriate, invite the child to tell a story about the animals using the pictures.

· · · · · Puzzling Nature · · · · ·

Materials Needed: pictures of forests, construction paper, scissors, glue, laminating material

Directions: The green, green forests in North America are certainly a showcase of beauty. Look for pictures of the temperate rain forests in the Pacific Northwest (Douglas fir trees), northern aspen-birch forests, loblolly or longleaf pine forests, or oak-hickory forests. The majestic trees of the forests are home to many different kinds of animals. Share some of the forest beauty through puzzles for the children to assemble. Mount each picture on white construction paper, leaving room for a border. Use a different colored marker to color the border of each puzzle. The child can sort the pieces by looking at the different colored borders. This helps the child to learn to look for color clues when working on a puzzle. In the center encourage the children to assemble the puzzles and then talk about the pictures. Have them explain how these forest pictures are similar and different.

· · · · · In the Forest · · · · ·

Materials Needed: books about the forest, puppets

Directions: Collect a variety of books about temperate forests in North America. Also gather puppets of animals that live in the forest. If these are not available, someone may be able to make paper bag puppets for the children to use in the center. Let the children "read" the books and tell stories about the animals.

Life in the Forest

owl

deer

oak tree

woodpecker

squirrel

lichens

mouse

pine tree

acorns

snail

spider

salamander

Five Furry Chipmunks

Five furry chipmunks
We simply adore.
One hid behind a branch,
Then there were _____.

Four furry chipmunks
Were climbing up a tree.
One slid to the ground,
Then there were _____.

Three furry chipmunks
Found an old shoe.
One crawled inside of it,
Then there were _____.

Two furry chipmunks
Were chasing in the sun.
One got tired and rested,
Then there were _____.

One furry chipmunk
Wanted to run—so,
ABRACADABRA!
Then there was _____.

—Louise Binder Scott

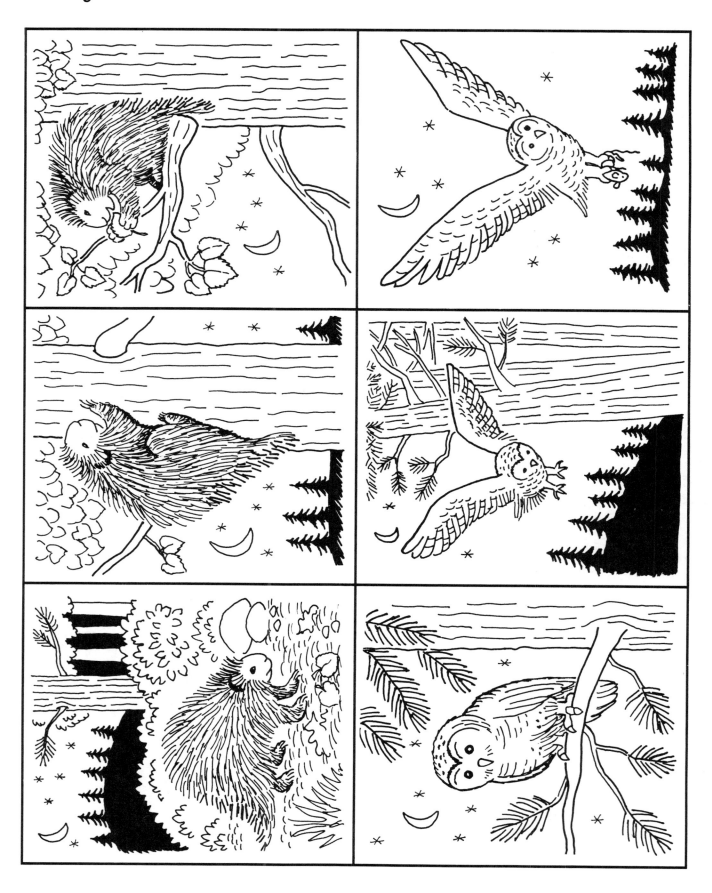

WRITING CENTER ACTIVITIES

· · · · · A "T" for Tall Trees · · · · ·

Materials Needed: large brown construction paper, white chalk, green tissue paper, index cards, scissors, paper cutter, marker, brown paper scraps, pencil, glue, paintbrush

Directions: The beautiful green tree is like a tall "T" in the forest as it blocks the sunshine with its canopy. With minimal preparation the materials can be ready for making colorful "T"s. To get started, outline a large bold-shaped "T" on each sheet of brown construction paper with white chalk. Make a set of word cards for each child by making dashed-shaped letters for the words "green" and "brown" on separate cards. Using the paper cutter, cut a large number of 3" (76 mm) tissue paper squares. In the center have the child brush glue on the top portion of the "T" and then place tissue paper on the glue. (Add a small amount of water to thin the glue.) When finished, have the child trace over the letters on the word cards and glue a few green "leaves" near the word "green" and a piece of brown construction paper near the word "brown." Remind the children that the letter "T" is like a tall tree. Your classroom will certainly change into a forest with these beautiful decorations.

· · · · · Forest Rubbings · · · · ·

Materials Needed: stencils, white construction paper, crayons, nature magazines, scissors, paste

Directions: In the forest there are many interesting animals and plants. Let the child cut out a favorite picture and make a rubbing of the first letter in its name. Finish the project by pasting the picture on the paper. Encourage the child to add more crayon rubbings and pictures to fill the construction paper.

Variation: To make a special decoration for the center, provide a rubbing of the word "forest" and glue pictures around the word to make an interesting miniature mural.

• • • • • A Walk in the Forest • • • • •

Materials Needed: pencils, scissors, paste, construction paper, patterns on pages 153 and 159, stapler

Directions: Let's take a walk in the green, green forest. What can you see? Just look at each booklet page to find out what it might be. This activity only requires the booklet page pattern and the pictures of animals from the lotto board pattern. To provide the materials make several copies of the booklet page for each child. In the center, have the child select an animal from the picture page and glue it on the booklet page. Have the child complete the sentence before selecting another animal for the next page in her booklet. If appropriate, let the children clip pictures from magazines or draw pictures for their booklets. To decorate the cover, print the title "A Walk in the Forest." Finish the decoration by making a crayon rubbing of leaves. (If possible, the child may work on the cover for the booklet during the "Forest Rubbings" activity.) When finished, bind the booklet pages with the construction paper cover.

• • • • • Tracing Fun • • • • •

Materials Needed: forest materials (leaves, sticks, pieces of bark), pencils, paper, crayons

Directions: Here is an interesting fine motor activity. To set up the center, gather materials from a wooded area and place them in a storage container. Encourage the child to select an item and trace around its shape on the paper. When finished, have the child add any distinguishing details.

• • • • • All About Forests • • • • •

Materials Needed: paper, pencils, magazines, paste, scissors, crayons

Directions: Paper, wood for burning and medicines are some of the products that come from forests. There is so much to tell about the importance of a forest. Invite the child to make a booklet about forests. The child may write and draw pictures about things he has learned. Encourage the child to borrow items from the science center that interest him for making rubbings, such as leaves, pine needles, and tree bark. When finished, he can include these rubbings in his booklet.

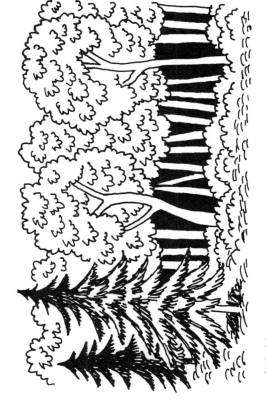

What can you see in
the green, green
forest?

I see a
looking at me!

MATH CENTER ACTIVITIES

· · · · · Footprints on the Trail · · · · ·

Materials Needed: tempera paint, old pair of tennis shoes, paper, large tray, marker

Directions: Have you ever counted your footsteps as you walked to a specific place? For this activity pretend you are walking down an imaginary path to the forest. To prepare the materials, locate an old pair of tennis shoes. Using tempera paint, make left and right prints on paper, approximately 20 to 30 shoe prints. Cut out the prints and mount them on construction paper. Write a numeral on each shoe print. (*Note:* You may wish to laminate these prints for durability.) In the center let the child work with a partner and place the prints in numerical order to lead you into the "forest." If you celebrate 100th day of the school year have the children work in teams and set up a path with 100 shoe prints. Let the children make the prints in the art center.

· · · · · Squirrels and Acorns · · · · ·

Materials Needed: patterns on page 162, self-sealing plastic bags, acorns, markers, scissors, construction paper, spring clothespins

Directions: These squirrels are very hungry; they love to eat acorns from the white oak tree. Decide how many acorns each squirrel can eat. To prepare the materials, collect acorns for the children to count or use the acorn pattern to make piles and piles of acorns. Decide if you would like the children either to count the acorns the squirrel is holding or place the corresponding number of acorns in the squirrel's basket. Also determine which sets of numbers the children need to practice in counting—such as sets of 5 to 10, 10 to 15, or 15 to 20. Make six photocopies of the squirrel and as many acorns as needed. If you would like the child to count sets of acorns, write the corresponding numerals on the clothespins. Decorate each clothespin with an acorn. If the child is creating the sets, either print a numeral on the squirrel or attach a clothespin that displays a numeral to each squirrel. Now the materials are ready and the children can count acorns. There are many other forest items the children can count and use to make sets. You may decide to change the activity by supplying different items to place in the squirrel's basket.

· · · · · Tall, Taller, Tallest Trees · · · · ·

Materials Needed: picture card patterns on page 163, construction paper, scissors, glue

Directions: Here is an activity for arranging the trees from smallest to largest or vice versa.

Enlarge and photocopy the pattern page on large copier paper and mount it on construction paper. Cut apart the picture cards and color them as desired. In the center the child may decide how to arrange the cards according to the size of the trees.

Variation: Other items can be arranged according to size. The children may be interested in arranging various pinecones or leaves by size.

· · · · · Measure and Compare Forest Animals · · · · ·

Materials Needed: patterns on page 164, opaque projector, pencil, large sheets of paper, scissors, tempera paint, construction paper, bulletin board paper, laminating material

Directions: Just how many chipmunks tall is a white-tailed deer? Are your young learners taller than the deer? These questions can be investigated by your students. To prepare the materials for the activity, reproduce about 20 copies of the chipmunk and mount them on construction paper. Cut out the chipmunks and laminate for durability. *Note:* To help the children understanding the actual size of these animals, make the chipmunk 8–10 inches (203–254 mm) in length and the white-tailed deer 4 ft. or 122 cm tall at the shoulder. Use the opaque projector to enlarge the deer pattern on bulletin board paper. After tracing the outline of the deer, paint it with tempera paint. Display the deer on a wall close to the floor. Provide the children with opportunities to compare their heights with the deer. Let them measure the deer with the chipmunk cutouts. Encourage the children to investigate their lengths while lying on the floor by measuring themselves with the chipmunk cutouts. This is an excellent opportunity for children to make comparisons.

· · · · · Weigh and Compare · · · · ·

Materials Needed: bucket balance, small logs, acorns, leaves, plastic containers, bathroom scale

Directions: Children can plan their own investigations with weights. Let them choose which items to weigh. Have them make predictions before weighing the items. Let the children set the items in the bucket balance and make comparisons. Some children may be interested in working with three different containers of acorns and arranging them by weight from heaviest to lightest or vice versa.

Variation: Encourage the children to find out how much squirrels or chipmunks weigh and compare their weights with containers of acorns. To set up the materials, supply a bag of acorns that matches the weight of the animal.

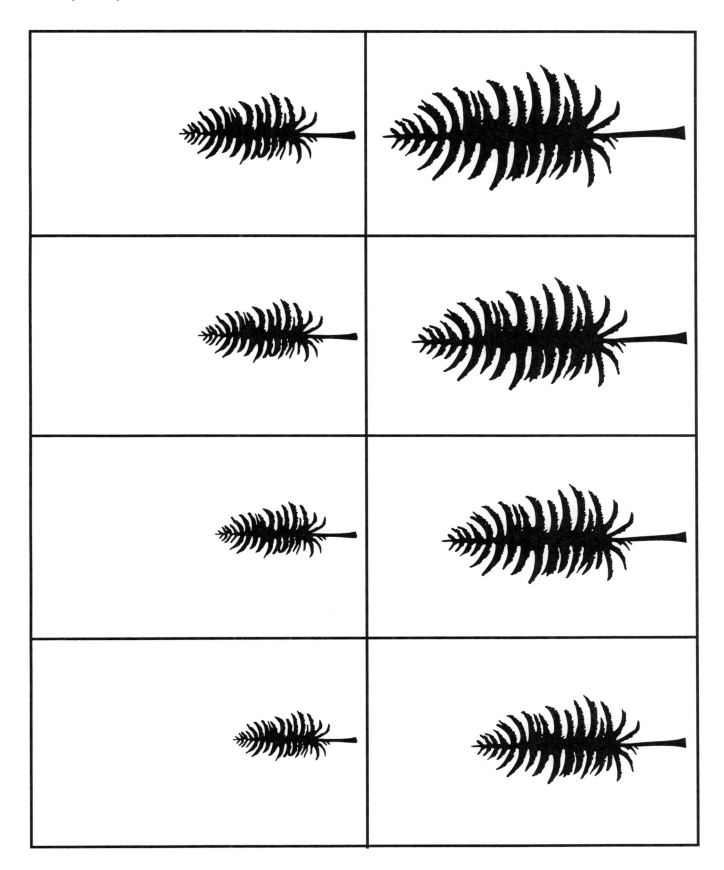

SCIENCE CENTER ACTIVITIES

· · · · · Sensory Exploration · · · · ·

Materials Needed: forest items and plastic objects (snake, spider and egg) to match pictures, picture card pattern on page 167, small box, construction paper, markers, scissors, utility knife, glue, mystery objects for treasure, large envelope

Directions: Let's search for hidden treasures but not travel too far. Just use your senses of sight and touch to find objects in the forest treasure box that correspond with picture cards. To make your forest treasure box, locate a box with a lid and cut a hole large enough for the child's hand to be inserted through it. Now gather objects that match the pictures on the pattern page. Place the items in the box. Photocopy the pattern page and mount it on construction paper. Cut apart the cards and place them in an envelope. In the center, encourage the child to work with a partner. Before the children search for objects in the box, reassure them that the egg, snake and spider are plastic toys. Have each child take a turn selecting a picture card and then trying to find the item in the box by using the sense of touch. After the children have played the game, you may wish to add one or two surprises (not pictured) for them to find and try to identify when they play the game a second time.

· · · · · Forest Animal Tracks · · · · ·

Materials Needed: picture card patterns on page 168–169, construction paper, scissors, glue

Directions: Many forest animals are active at night. This makes it difficult for a person to find them during the day. Help the child understand that we can tell a story about the animals by looking for tracks on the ground. Prepare the picture cards by photocopying them and mounting them on construction paper. Color the pictures as desired and then cut them apart. In the center, encourage the child to look closely at each animal's feet to match the tracks with the animal. Arrange the cards to show the matches.

Variation: Perhaps the children would like to look for tracks in sand, dirt or snow. Try to locate tracks that have been made by animals the children can recognize.

····· Classification Fun ·····

Materials Needed: rocks, leaves, acorns, pieces of tree bark, pinecones and other forest items

Directions: Gather a variety of natural items. Be sure to include several samples of each kind of item. In the center the child may work with a partner and sort the items by kind, size, texture, color, living/nonliving, and so on. Encourage the children to sort the objects one way. Discuss the results with them and then let the children sort the items in a different way.

····· Forest Observations ·····

Materials Needed: various items from wooded areas (moss, samples of tree bark, leaves, dirt, decaying leaves, pinecones, lichens on branches, log sliced to show growth rings, different kinds of pine needles, decaying pine needles, land snails and insects), magnifying glass, pencil, paper, plastic jars with lids, construction paper, crayons

Directions: There is so much for a child to observe when examining forest items. In the science center, create a touch and feel mini-museum for the children to explore. Encourage them to compare and contrast pinecones, pine needles, leaves, and tree bark. The children may also be interested in investigating growth rings on logs, observing how a land snail moves and feeds, comparing moss with lichens, and so on. Now is a perfect time for the children to write about what they are learning and observing.

····· Concentrating on Animals ·····

Materials Needed: patterns on page 170, construction paper, scissors, glue, markers, books about forest animals

Directions: This memory match game is easy to play but remember that not all of these animals can be seen in the forest at the same time. Some animals hunt for food at night while others are active during the day. To prepare the game pieces reproduce the pattern page and mount the copy on construction paper. If you prefer large-size playing cards, enlarge the pattern page before photocopying it. Color the animals if desired and cut apart the cards. *Note:* Refer to a reference guide for exact coloration and markings. Children can play this memory game with partners. To begin play, turn the picture cards *face down* and mix them before arranging the cards in two rows of four each. Each player must turn two cards *face up* to make a match. If a match is made the player keeps the cards. If a match is not made the cards are turned *face down*. Play continues until all matches are made.

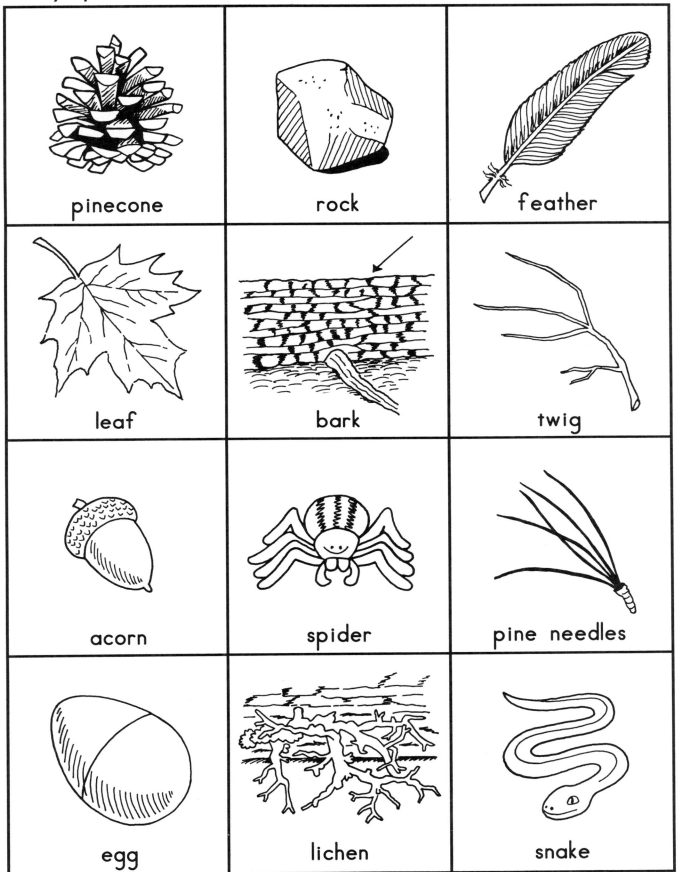

pinecone	rock	feather
leaf	bark	twig
acorn	spider	pine needles
egg	lichen	snake

Animal Tracks Picture Card Patterns

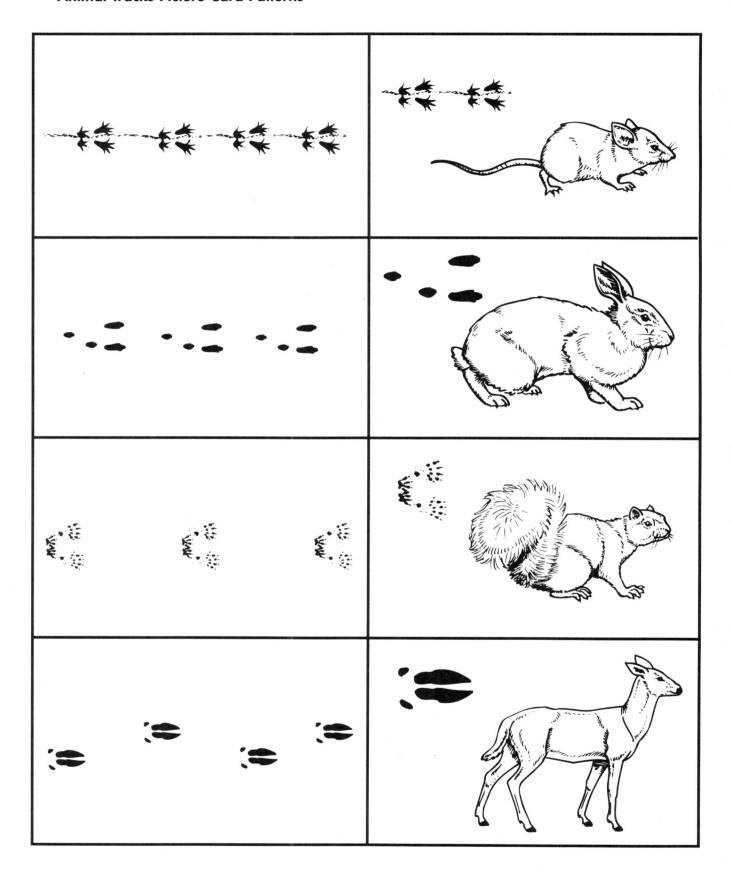

Animal Tracks Picture Card Patterns

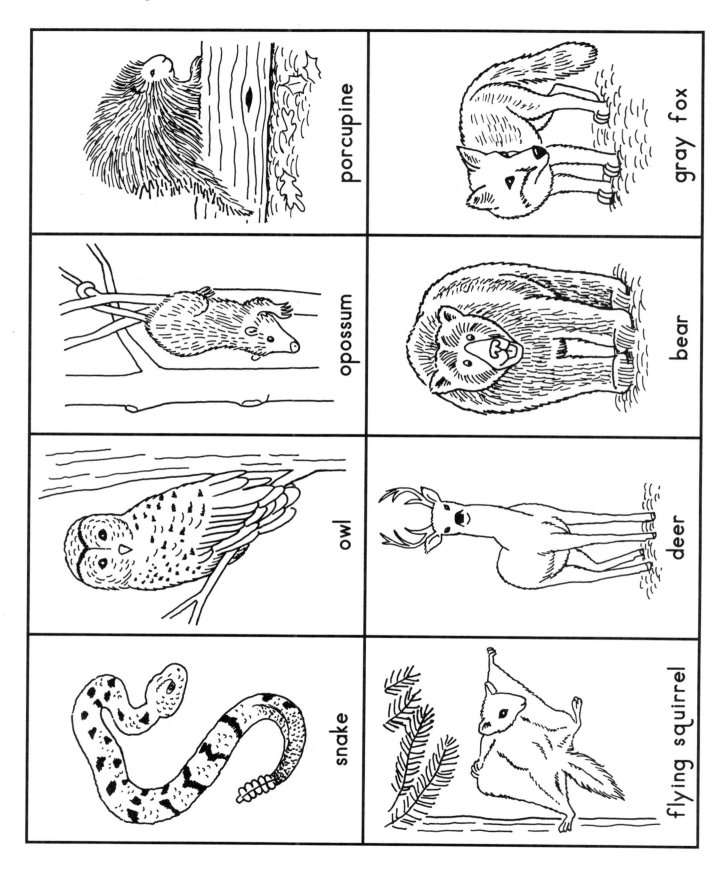

porcupine

gray fox

opossum

bear

owl

deer

snake

flying squirrel

ART CENTER ACTIVITIES

· · · · · Nature Prints · · · · ·

Materials Needed: leaves, sticks, samples of bark, pinecones, acorns, other seeds from trees, bunches of pine needles, tempera paints, Styrofoam trays, paper, large brown paper bags

Directions: Nature prints are wonderful for decorating the classroom and home. Children can create prints on construction paper or brown paper bags that have been cut open to make them lay flat. To make the prints, gather natural items from a wooded area. Spread a small amount of paint on a Styrofoam tray, a different color on each tray. Let the child dip the object in the paint and then press it against the paper to transfer a print. Lift the object and then place it in a different spot and press. This time the print has less paint but you can still identify it. Encourage the child to continue dipping objects in paint and making prints until she is pleased with the design.

· · · · · Nature Collage · · · · ·

Materials Needed: natural objects from wooden areas, construction paper, glue, tissue paper (blue, green, brown), glue

Directions: Beautiful collages can be made by gluing natural objects on a tissue paper background. To begin the project, have the child paint the paper with glue that has been thinned with water. After the glue is brushed on the paper, tear pieces of tissue paper and flatten them in the glue with a paintbrush. Allow this to dry. Encourage the child to finish the collage by gluing natural objects onto the paper to create a nature collage.

· · · · · Stick Painting · · · · ·

Materials Needed: thick tempera paint, finger paint paper, sticks, piece of cardboard

Directions: Instead of a paintbrush use a stick to paint a picture. After gathering the materials, encourage the child to cover the paper with paint by spreading it evenly with the edge of a piece of cardboard. Before the paint dries, let the child use a stick to draw images or designs in the paint. Set the painting aside to air dry before displaying it in the classroom.

• • • • • Seed Designs • • • • •

Materials Needed: lightweight cardboard or poster board, glue, seeds, pencil, pinecones

Directions: Delightful seed designs can be made with natural objects from a wooded area. To prepare for this activity, gather interesting materials that the children may use by gluing them on the cardboard to make attractive designs.

• • • • • Green, Green Forest Scenes • • • • •

Materials Needed: tempera paints, paper, art easel, paintbrushes, smock

Directions: Wonderful forest scenes can be painted on the art easel. To provide different colors that you might see in a forest, mix several shades of green by adding yellow to green and blue to green. Also mix several shades of brown by adding red, yellow or blue. Place the new paint colors along with the red, yellow and blue in the art center. Let the children paint forest scenes and later display the paintings for others to admire.

Variation: The children might like to use a screen and work with splatter paint to create forest foliage. Have them start by painting tree trunks and then let them add the "greenery" by splattering paint through a screen. To do this, brush a paint-covered toothbrush across the screen which is held above the paper.

OUR GARDEN PATCH

Caring for plants is a pleasant pastime for many people. Hopefully, this enjoyment will be experienced by the children in your classroom. This theme offers a host of activities that are related to plants. However, the best part will be setting up a small garden patch in your classroom. To do this, transform a small wading pool or your water or sand table into a miniature garden. This cooperative project helps children understand the process of planting and taking care of plants. Decide the location of your garden and select the seeds for planting. Perhaps you are only interested in working with very small gardens, then consider large plastic containers that have drain holes on the bottoms. To get started, place small rocks and sand in the bottom of the container for the drainage of water away from the plants' roots, then fill the container with potting soil. Select plants that will be small in size unless you are planning on transplanting them into larger containers or setting them in the ground. To plant the seeds follow the instructions on the packages; some seeds must be placed on the surface of the soil while others are covered with dirt. After the seeds are planted, note the amount of time that is needed for germination. This information is included on the package. To help the children understand that seeds need time to develop, record on poster board the name of the plant (or glue the seed packet in place) and show with "X"s the average number of days for germination. Repeat the process for all plants sown in your garden patch. To track the germination time, each day have a child circle an "X" and look for seedlings. When the child notices that the seeds of a particular plant are sprouting, place a star on the corresponding "X." Continue observing for signs of growth. As the plants grow and mature in your garden patch, the children can observe changes, measure growth and marvel at plant life.

As you set up your centers in the classroom, be sure to include books about garden plants and related occupations for the children to "read" in your library corner. During group time talk about gardens and plant life or read aloud informative picture books, such as:
- Ehlert, Lois. *Growing Vegetable Soup.* Harcourt Brace Jovanovich, 1987.
- King, Elizabeth. *The Pumpkin Patch.* Dutton Children's Books, 1990.
- McMillan, Bruce. *Growing Colors.* Lothrop, Lee & Shepard, 1988.

· · · · · The Dramatic Play Center · · · · ·

Change this area into a nursery, greenhouse or vegetable stand. For a vegetable stand, convert a large refrigerator box into a stand. Cut an opening for the display area and attach another piece of cardboard for the awning. Paint it as desired. Gather gardening-related items, play money, plastic plants and foods, paper, markers, crayons, and craft sticks.

ACTIVITIES FOR CURRICULUM AREAS

READING & LANGUAGE DEVELOPMENT CENTER ACTIVITIES

····· From Seed to Food Stand ·····

Materials Needed: patterns on page 177, scissors, construction paper, glue, markers

Directions: So much happens in the garden patch before the produce is sold at the stand. Look at the picture cards and then tell the story about growing vegetables. The center materials can be easily assembled by reproducing the picture cards pattern. You may wish to enlarge the pictures to fit on 11" x 17" (279 x 432 mm) paper. Mount the photocopy on construction paper and color the pictures as desired. Cut apart the cards and place them in the center. Encourage the child to work with a partner. Let the children talk about the pictures before arranging them in sequential order. When finished, ask them to share their stories about the pictures.

Variation: Gather catalogs and spring and summer magazine issues for use in the center. Encourage the children to make their own story cards by clipping pictures and gluing them on large pieces of construction paper. Their stories can be about imaginary gardens or about taking care of their small garden patches. If the children are telling about personal experiences, encourage them to draw pictures that show themselves working with the plants.

····· What's Growing in the Patch? ·····

Materials Needed: picture card patterns on page 178, scissors, construction paper, glue, markers, cassette tape, tape recorder and player

Directions: It is always fun to talk about what is growing in the garden patch. You may wish to share this finger play during group time. To prepare the center materials, print the finger play on poster board. Photocopy the picture cards and mount them on construction paper. Then cut apart the cards and color them as desired. Adhere Velcro buttons on the chart at the end of each line and also on the back of the picture cards. Provide a recording of the rhyme. In the center, have the child listen to the rhyme and then arrange the pictures in sequential order (the picture with a star is first). When finished, ask the child to tell you which words at the end of the lines rhyme.

> **Things That Grow**
> Here is my little garden bed.
> Here is one tomato ripe and red.
> Here are two great long string beans.
> Here are three bunches of spinach greens.
> Here are four cucumbers on a vine.
> This little garden is all mine.
> *-Adapted from Louise Binder*

····· Puzzling About Gardening ·····

Materials Needed: patterns on pages 179–180, construction paper, scissors, glue, markers

Directions: Here are some puzzles that might challenge young gardeners. To prepare the puzzles enlarge the pattern page to fit on 11" x 17" (279 x 432 mm) copier paper. Mount the pictures on construction paper and color them as desired. Cut apart the cards and then cut each picture along the dashed line. In order to assemble the miniature puzzles, encourage the child to look at the pictures and the words. When the child is matching the labeled picture with the corresponding word, it is not expected that the child can read the word. This activity is only meant to increase awareness of print.

Variation: Other puzzles can be made by collecting large pictures of flowers and gardening tools from magazines and catalogs. Mount the pictures on construction paper and then cut them apart.

····· Foods and Plants Memory Match Game ·····

Materials Needed: nursery and seed catalogs (identical pairs), index cards or construction paper, markers, scissors, glue

Directions: A wealth of catalog pictures are yours to use when creating memory match games. To prepare the picture cards, cut out identical pairs of pictures from nursery and seed catalogs. Mount the pictures on index cards or construction paper. Children can play this memory game with partners. To begin play, turn the picture cards *face down* and mix them before arranging the cards in two or three rows. Each player must turn two cards *face up* to make a match. If a match is made the player keeps the cards. If a match is not made the cards are turned *face down*. Play continues until all matches are made.

····· Garden Patch Sounds ·····

Materials Needed: mat pattern on pages 181–182, poster board, scissors, glue, markers, milk jug caps (or poster board circles), black permanent marker

Directions: Out in the garden patch you can find many fascinating plants and animals. Look closely at this scene and identify the initial consonant sounds for objects. To prepare the materials, transfer the game board pattern to 11" x 17" (279 x 432 mm) copier paper by enlarging the images at 120%. Color the scene and mount it on poster board by gluing the sections together. Here are some of the initial consonant sounds that are covered in this activity: c–carrots, b–bird, d–daisies, f–fence, l–lettuce, m–marigolds and mouse, p–peas and pot, r–rabbit, s–sunflowers, t–tomatoes, w–water, and z–zucchini. Print these letters on the milk jug caps. In the center let the child complete the matches by placing each letter near the corresponding item in the scene.

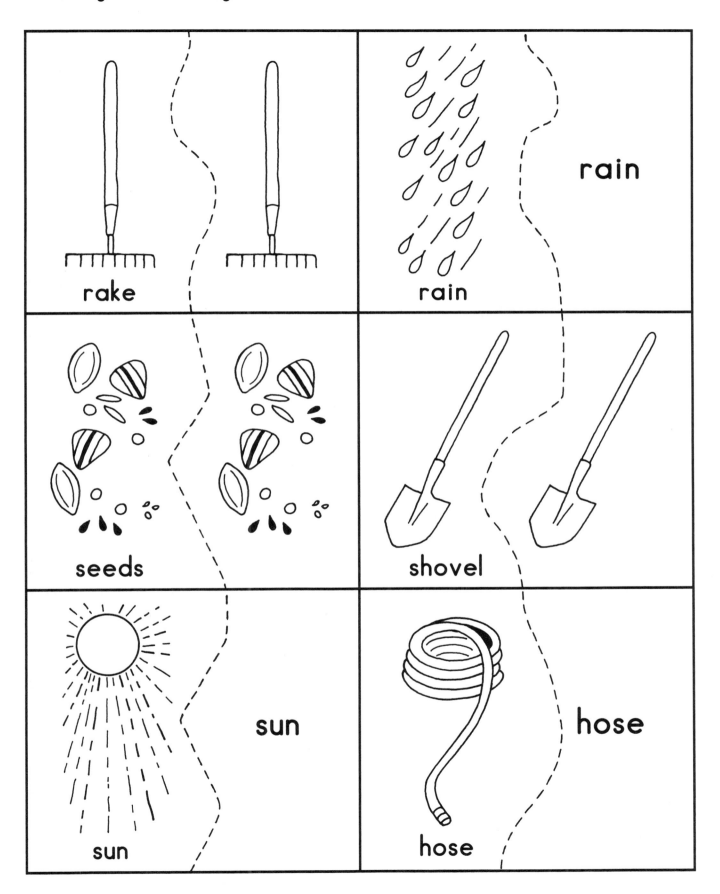

rake

rain

seeds

shovel

sun

hose

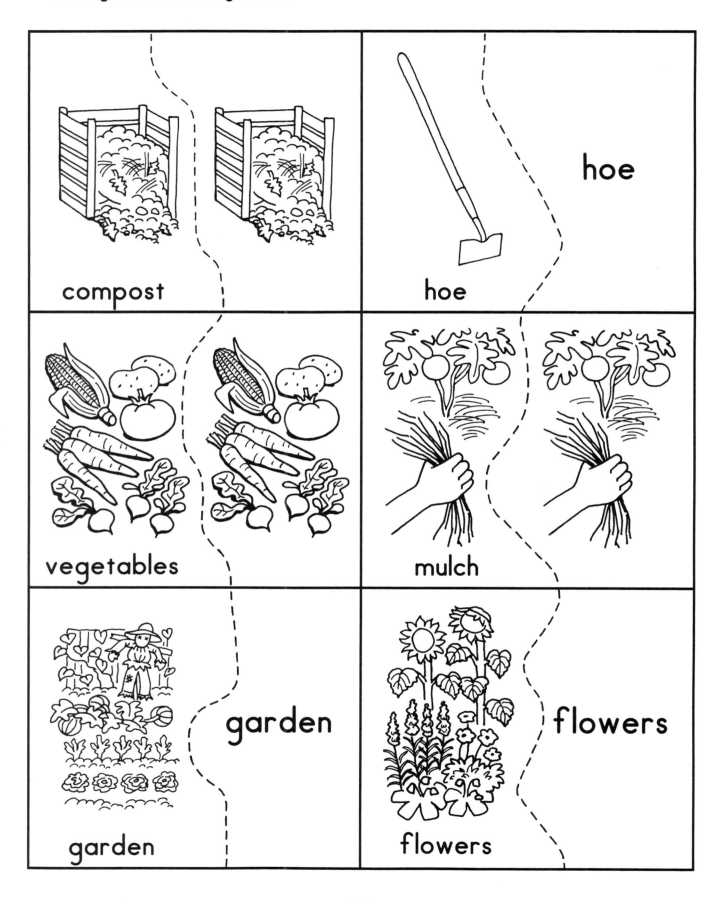

compost

hoe

hoe

vegetables

mulch

garden

garden

flowers

flowers

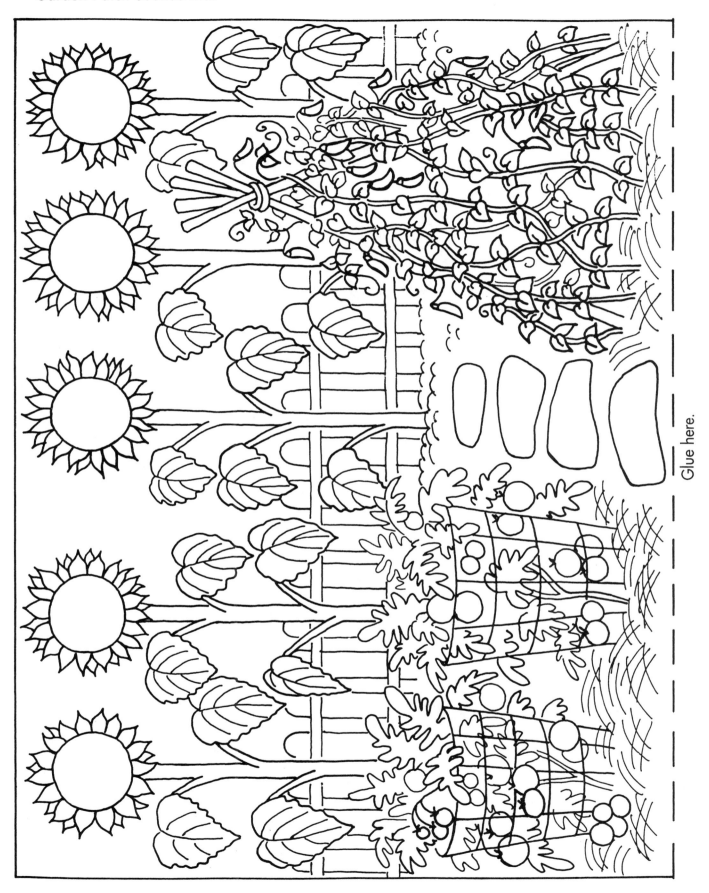

Glue here.

WRITING CENTER ACTIVITIES

· · · · · Pictures and Words · · · · ·

Materials Needed: poster board, empty seed packets, seed catalogs, nursery catalogs, scissors, glue, pencils, paper, index cards, markers, colored pencils, crayons

Directions: Prepare a word bank by printing the names of vegetables, fruits, garden tools, environmental words, animals that visit a garden (insects, birds, mammals, frogs, snakes), and others on poster board. If possible try to locate pictures for the words to make a pictorial chart. Display empty seed packets as decorations in the center. Supply paper, a pattern page that looks like a seed packet, index cards, and other paper materials for the child to use when printing words, drawing pictures, writing sentences about what is happening in the classroom, and so on.

· · · · · My Garden Patch Book · · · · ·

Materials Needed: booklet pattern on page 185, pictures for booklet on pages 186 (tomato) and 192, scissors, pencils, paste, paper

Materials Needed: Watch out! Something is popping out of this garden. Children can work cooperatively or individually making copies of this pop-up book. To create this book about vegetables that are grown in a garden patch, reproduce six copies of the pattern page and fold them in half. Cut two slits in the paper to make a tab as shown. (Cut on the dashed lines.) Fold the paper tab forward to make a new crease. Open the paper and push the paper tab to make it look like the example shown. Repeat the steps for the other pop-up pages. Glue or staple the pages together as shown. Have the children finish each page by completing the sentence and gluing a picture on the tab. See pages 186 (tomato) and 192 for pictures that can be used in the booklet or clip pictures from seed catalogs.

· · · · · Lacing Shapes · · · · ·

Materials Needed: shoelace or yarn, masking tape, poster board, patterns on page 186, scissors, glue, markers, hole punch

Directions: Young learners will delight in lacing these shapes that can be seen in a garden patch.

To prepare the materials for this fine motor skill activity, enlarge and reproduce the flower, butterfly and rabbit. Mount the copies on poster board. Cut out the shapes and color them as desired. Punch holes along the outer edges of the cutouts. Cut pieces of yarn 18" (457 mm) in length. Wrap masking tape around one end of each string. Tie the other end of the string to the cutout. These delightful shapes are now ready for lacing.

· · · · · All About Purple and Pink · · · · ·

Materials Needed: pattern on page 187, purple construction paper, white construction paper, scissors, tissue paper, paste, stapler, seed catalogs, nursery catalogs, poster board

Directions: What do you think about purple and pink? This question is answered by cutting out pictures of objects in these colors. When finished, the children will have a booklet to share with others. To prepare the materials, make two copies of the pattern page for each child. In the center encourage the child make the booklet by pasting or drawing pictures of flowers, eggplant, fruits, gardening clothes or tools that show the featured colors. In order to finish the booklet the child must trace over the words "purple" and "pink." If the child has any opinions about these colors be sure to encourage him to write about them in the booklet. The cover of the booklet can be decorated with purple and pink tissue paper squares that are cut on the paper cutter. Finally, bind the cover with the booklet pages into an adorable book.

Variation: A large "Pp" can be made as a center decoration. Just draw large, wide outlines of the letters on white construction paper. Have the child decorate the letter with purple and pink tissue paper squares that are rolled into berries and glued in place.

· · · · · Red Like Beet Juice · · · · ·

Materials Needed: beet root juice, small paintbrush, bulletin board paper, smock, white bulletin board paper, plastic sheet, vinegar

Directions: It is such a treat to print with beets. How can this be? Use beet root juice as a natural dye. Add a small amount of vinegar to the juice. The color red is a marvelous color when thinking about food—raspberries, radishes, beets, and tomatoes. These different shades of red are a wonderful part of the garden rainbow. Children can find out how beet root juice stains paper by using it to print their names. Begin the mural by printing the word "red" in large letters in the center of the paper. *Note:* Be sure to place a plastic sheet under the paper to prevent staining the floor or table. Have the children print their names in random places. The children also may print words or thoughts with the beet juice.

Variation: Try other natural dyes when printing on paper.

In my _arden I can _ee

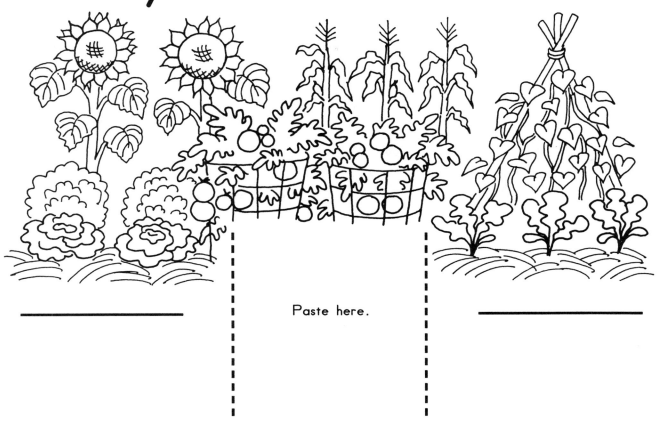

_____   Paste here.   _____

just for _e.

186

Purple is

Pink is

I think

What do
you think
about
purple
and
pink?

MATH CENTER ACTIVITIES

····· Measuring a Giant ·····

Materials Needed: patterns on page 190, bulletin board paper, markers, scissors, paper, math counters, *Optional:* cobs of rainbow corn, sunflower seed head, part of a sunflower stalk

Directions: How big is a sunflower? How many corn cobs tall is this giant plant? These are some questions your young learners can explore by using nonstandard measurements. To set up the center, enlarge the corn cobs and then reproduce about 24 copies. Mount them on construction paper. Cut out the corn cobs. If you prefer that the child work with smaller numbers, make the corn cobs 10–12 inches (254–305 mm) in length. Because the sunflower plant can be 12 ft. or 3.7 m tall, use the opaque projector to enlarge the sunflower to actual size on bulletin board paper. After tracing the outline of the plant, paint it with tempera paint. Display the plant on a wall close to the floor. Measure the plant with string and tape the string to the floor along a wall so the children will not trip on the string. Provide the children with opportunities to discover how much shorter they are than the plant. Also encourage them to measure the string with small corn cob cutouts or actual corn cobs. This giant plant which grows in the patch truly is fascinating.

Variations: Encourage the child to think about how many seeds are in the sunflower head. Let each child examine the seeds and remove 10 seeds for counting. Collect the seeds in a container and record the sets of 10. When 100 seeds have been collected, start filling a new container. If a scale is available, weigh the sunflower head before removing the seeds. Let the children compare their weights with the sunflower.

····· Pennies and Nickels to Earn ·····

Materials Needed: patterns on pages 191–192, scissors, construction paper, glue, play money or actual coins (pennies and nickels), markers

Directions: You can make cash when selling foods at the Garden Patch Stand. Actually this entertaining game reinforces how to exchange pennies for nickels as foods are sold. To set up this game, make three copies of the picture cards and a copy of the food stand as the game board. Mount the copies on construction paper. Color as desired. Cut apart the cards and place them along with the game board and coins in a tray. Be sure to print a card that states "Closed." Encourage the child to play with a partner and sell foods at the stand. To begin play, stack the cards *face up* in a pile on the stand. Each child draws a card and collects the corresponding number of pennies. For example, if the card shows three radishes, the child collects three pennies.

Discard the card by placing it in the "Sold Box." Play continues until a player has five pennies. The child then exchanges the pennies for a nickel and continues to take a turn by drawing a card. When the player collects four nickels that player stops taking a turn and lets the other player continue until finished. When both players each have four nickels or 20¢ the stand is closed. Now they can display the sign "Closed." If the players are interested in playing another game, just open the stand for business.

· · · · · Patterning with Seeds · · · · ·

Materials Needed: pattern on page 193, scissors, large seeds (two different kinds), construction paper, glue

Directions: Birds love seeds and so will your children with this delightful repeat patterning activity. Many interesting patterns can be made with seeds. To prepare the materials make two copies of the patterning board and mount them on construction paper. Decide which repeat patterns the children will finish. Glue the seeds in place to start the patterns, such as AABB, ABAB or ABBA patterns. Be sure to provide large interesting seeds for the children to use.

· · · · · Flowers to Count · · · · ·

Materials Needed: artificial flowers (different sizes), six empty frozen juice cans, decorative paper, glue, scissors, markers, paintbrush

Directions: More than vegetables can be grown in a garden patch. Many gardeners enjoy working with flowers. For this activity, prepare decorative vases for the flower arrangements by painting the juice cans with glue (thinned with water) and covering them with decorative paper. Cover the paper with another coat of the glue and then set the can aside to dry. Continue the process until you have decorated all of the cans. Decide how many flowers should be arranged in each can and then write the corresponding numeral on the can with a marker. Set the "vases" and flowers in the center. Now the children can arrange and rearrange the flowers to make interesting bouquets.

· · · · · Sunny Arrangements · · · · ·

Materials Needed: yellow poster board, scissors, pencil

Directions: Cut out identical pairs of suns (round circles) in four sizes from the poster board. Set the materials in the center. In the center, have the child arrange the yellow suns from largest to smallest or vice versa. Also provide a set of three suns each cut into halves, fourths, or thirds for the children to assemble. During group time introduce the children to fractions.

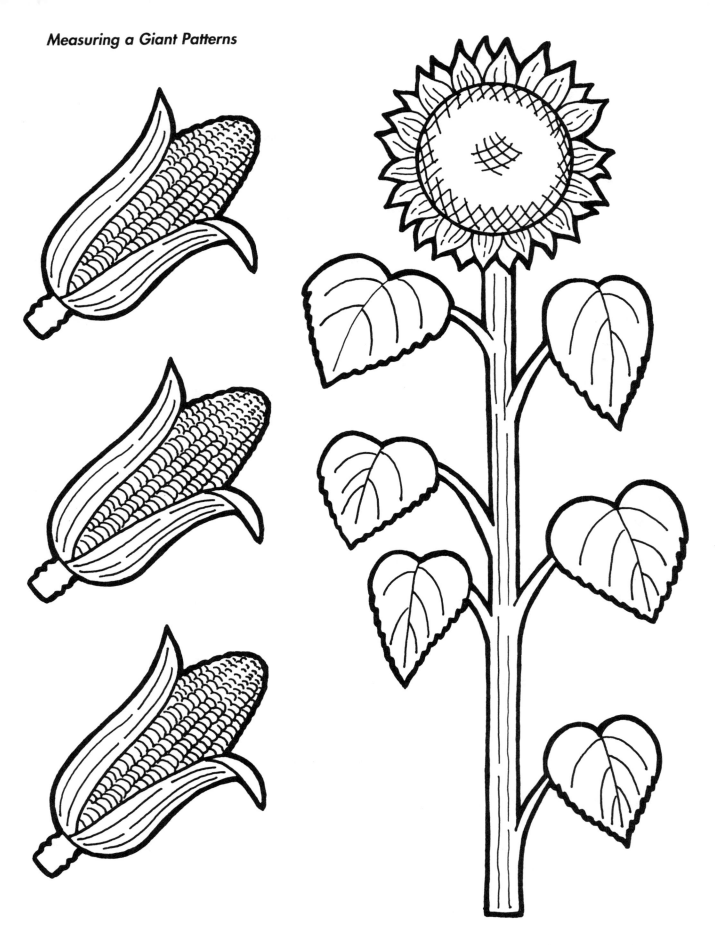

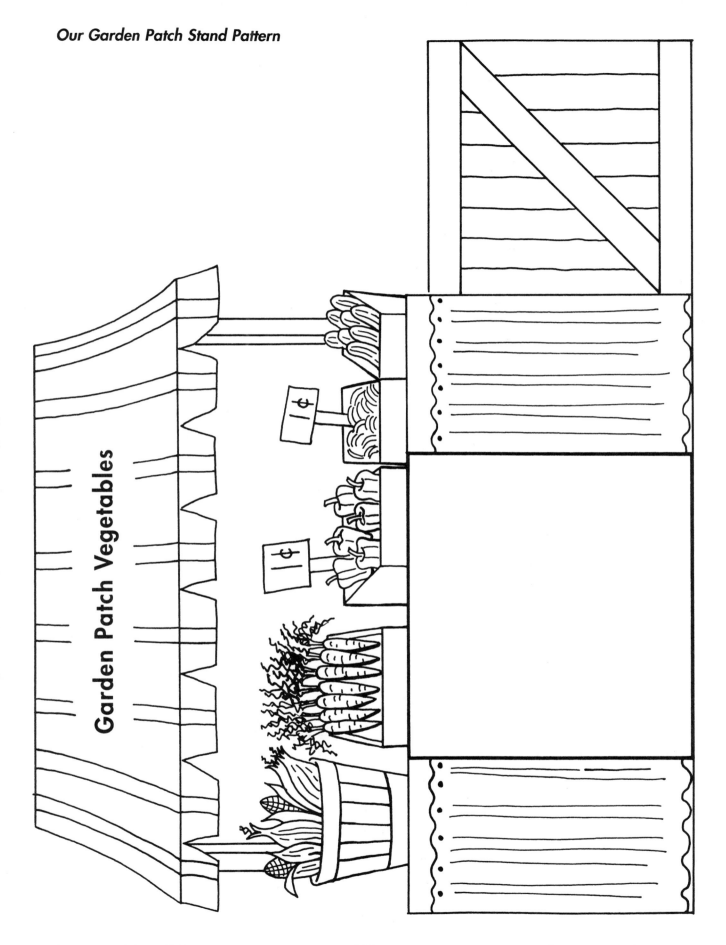

Garden Patch Vegetables

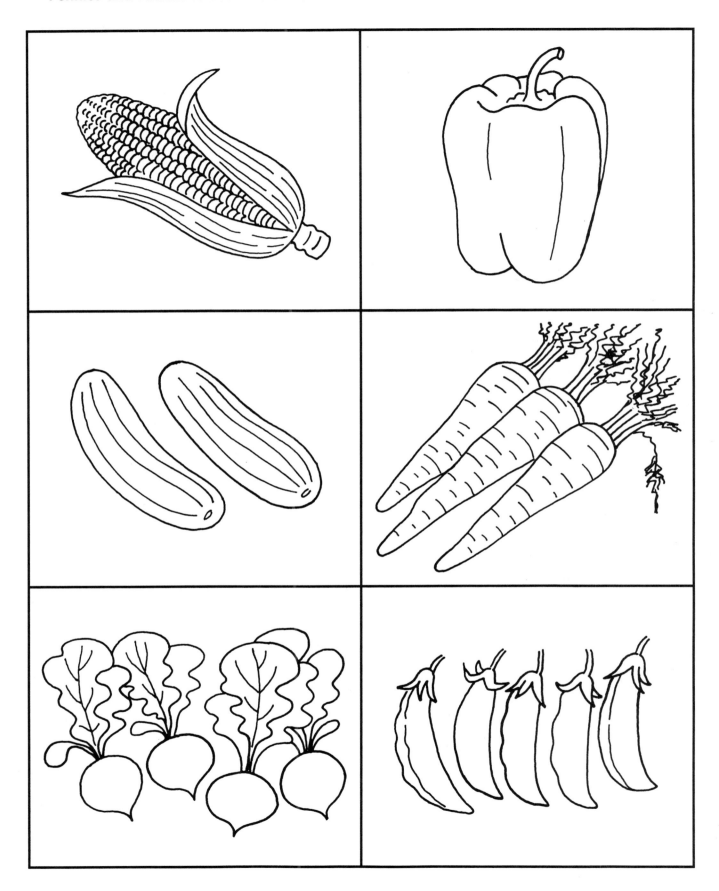

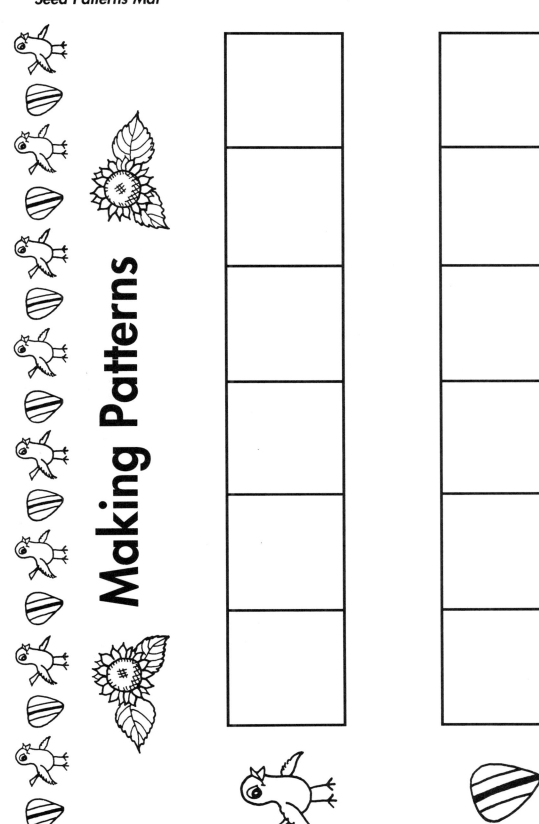

Making Patterns

SCIENCE CENTER ACTIVITIES

· · · · · Seed Discovery · · · · ·

Materials Needed: oranges, grapefruit, a mature cucumber or zucchini, green pepper, small squash or cantaloupe, magnifying glass, plastic knife, cutting knife for adult use, seed pods from flowers if available, large tray, plastic spoon, paper, pencil

Directions: Let's hunt for seeds in foods. Just search the produce section of a grocery store and vegetable stand for samples to use in the classroom. Also visit neighborhood gardens and ask for donations. Place the gathered items on a tray and set it on a tabletop. Cut the foods in half to show the seeds. Encourage the children to remove some seeds from the foods or seed pods and examine them.

Variation: If interested, allow the children to plant dried seeds in containers.

· · · · · Will It Grow? · · · · ·

Materials Needed: assorted seeds (beans, peas, grass, radishes, marigold, and other large flower and vegetable seeds), small sponges, shallow dishes, water, tiny pebbles, small manufactured objects, index cards, plastic bags, Styrofoam trays, marker, masking tape, magnifying lens, plastic wrap

Directions: Is it a seed? Will it grow? Children can examine the provided materials to determine which ones are seeds. To set up the materials for this activity, place a small assortment of seeds, pebbles and manufactured objects in a plastic bag for each child. Encourage the child to sort the objects and place on the sponge those items she thinks will grow. Set the sponge in the shallow dish and label the dish with masking tape. Let the child moisten the sponge and then set the dish away from direct sunlight. Cover the dish with plastic wrap to prevent the loss of moisture. Each day have the child watch for changes—the germination of the seeds. When the seeds have sprouted, have the child glue identical seeds on an index card to record which ones did grow.

Variation: If you would like the children to learn the names of a few seeds, provide empty seed packets or pictures along with the correct seeds. Glue the materials on a small section of tagboard. Provide additional seeds for the child to match with the corresponding seed packets. When the child is finished, have him tell a partner the name of each seed.

· · · · · Identifying the Parts of a Plant · · · · ·

Materials Needed: self-sealing plastic bags, radish seeds, paper towels, water, stapler, lotto board pattern on page 196, scissors, construction paper, glue, masking tape, marker

Direction: By learning the parts of the plant, children can identify them when observing plant growth in their mini-gardens. To prepare the materials, reproduce two copies of the pattern page and mount them on construction paper. Color the pictures as desired and then cut apart the picture cards on one copy. The second copy will be the lotto board. Gather the remaining materials to make mini-gardens in plastic bags. To do this, place a folded paper towel in the plastic bag like a sandwich. Staple the paper towel in place. (Refer to the illustration.)  Moisten the paper towel. Repeat the process for each pair of students. In the center the children can play with the lotto board by matching the pictures and practicing the names of the parts of a plant. When they are finished, they can place a few radish seeds in their plastic bag mini-gardens. The seeds must rest on the paper towel. Tape the mini-garden to a wall in a sunny area. Have the children watch for changes each day. *Note:* The seeds will germinate in two or three days. What an exciting time! Encourage the children to talk about the seedlings.

· · · · · Propagation Fun · · · · · ·

Materials Needed: plastic jars, coleus plant, water, scissors, picture card patterns on page 197, masking tape for labeling, marker, magnifying glass

Directions: No fuss, no mess with this activity! Locate a mature coleus plant, small plastic jars and scissors. Make a copy of the pattern page and mount it on construction paper. Cut apart the cards and place them with the gathered materials in the science center. Invite the child to follow the instruction cards to start a new plant. Encourage her to watch for roots to develop. Be sure to label her experiment. Invite the children to start other plants with plant parts. For example, work with a carrot top (pictured on card), radish top, potato, or tradescantia cutting (pictured on card).

· · · · · What Do Plants Need? · · · · ·

Materials Needed: three small identical potted plants for pairs of students, water, small boxes, masking tape, construction paper, pencils, glue

Directions: Does a plant need water and sunlight? How should you take care of a plant? Let the children investigate these questions. Provide plants for each team of children. Encourage them to not water the first plant, keep the second plant in the dark (water when necessary) by covering it with a box, and give the third plant proper care (water and sunlight). Have the children observe the plants once a day for changes.

Parts of a Plant

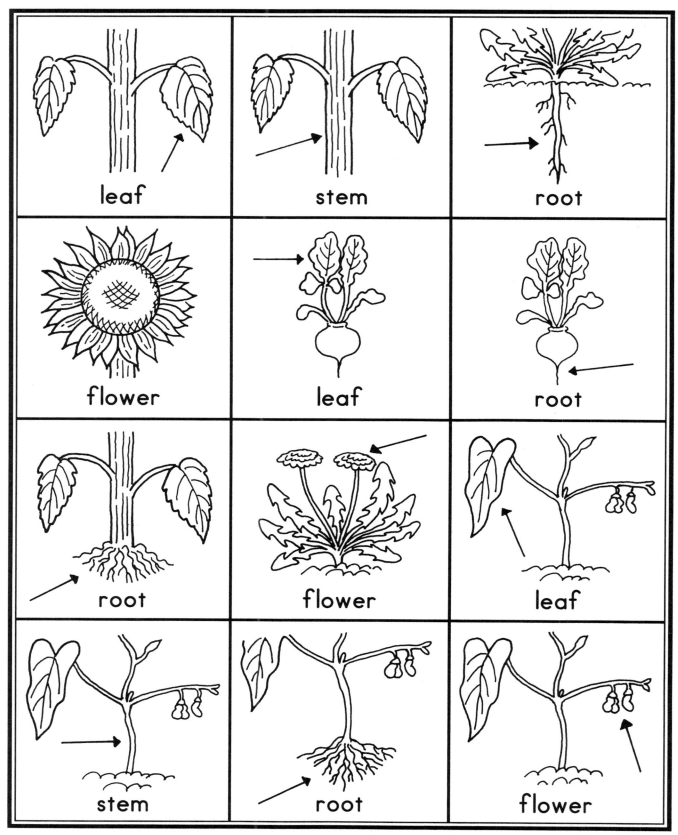

leaf	stem	root
flower	leaf	root
root	flower	leaf
stem	root	flower

Propagation Fun Picture Card Patterns

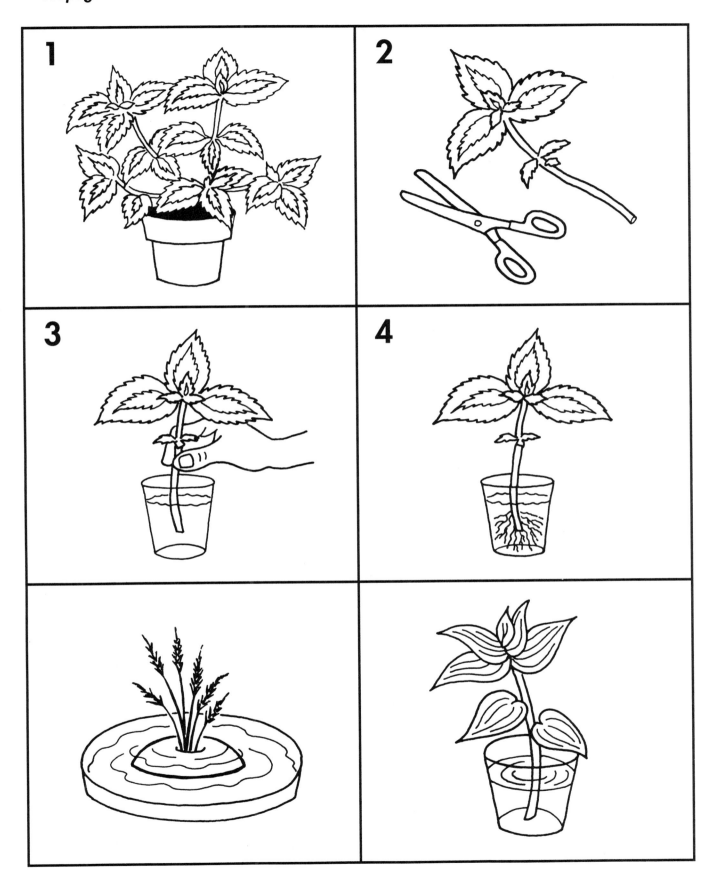

ART CENTER ACTIVITIES

· · · · · My Garden Patch · · · · ·

Materials Needed: tempera paints (various colors), paintbrushes, paper, smock, easel

Directions: Invite the child to paint a garden scene. When he is finished, have him tell you about his painting. Record these thoughts on a sentence strip which is displayed with the painting.

· · · · · Beautiful Prints · · · · ·

Materials Needed: tempera paints, Styrofoam trays, natural objects to print (apples, cauliflower florets, marigolds, pea pods), paper

Directions: Interesting prints can be made with natural objects. Pour a small amount of paint on a Styrofoam tray. Let the child dip an object, such as a cauliflower floret, in the paint and then gently press the object on the paper to leave a print. Repeat the process with different colors.

· · · · · Tissue Paper Flowers · · · · ·

Materials Needed: tissue paper (assorted colors), paper cutter, paper, glue, pencil, paintbrush

Directions: The children can create wonderful floral scenes with beautiful tissue paper colors. To prepare the materials, cut the tissue paper into small squares on a paper cutter. Show the children how to work with tissue paper by gluing on small "berries" or flat pieces.

· · · · · Veggie Sculptures · · · · ·

Materials Needed: project clay having vegetable colors (recipe on page 30), fresh vegetables, plastic knives

Directions: Prepare the clay according to the recipe. Encourage the children to use the clay to form vegetable shapes. Before they start have the children examine the fresh vegetables.

· · · · · Crayon Etchings · · · · ·

Materials Needed: crayons, 4½" x 6" (114 x 152 mm) drawing paper, craft sticks

Directions: Delightful crayon etchings are a wonderful way to show the beauty of a garden patch. To do this, have the children color their papers with patches of bright colors, completing covering the paper. When finished, encourage the children to cover the bright crayon colors with black. Finally, have the child use the craft stick to scratch a picture in the black, revealing the layer of bright colors.

A RAINBOW OF COLORS

Color is everywhere. Just look around and list all the colors you see. Actually there are over 10 million colors for everyone to enjoy. Some people have specific color preferences while others enjoy the majority of colors.

To prepare the classroom environment, hang colorful streamers throughout the room. Encourage the children to paint rainbow pictures and other colorful scenes for displaying in the room. If it is possible, obtain a parachute for gross motor activities. The children may be interested in participating in special color days by dressing in the featured color. Provide sugar cookies frosted with the coordinating color for treats. With a little imagination, this truly is a colorful experience for the children.

As you set up your centers, be sure to include books about colors and people who work with color for the children to "read" in your library corner. Share information about birthstones and featured colors for each month. During group time talk about how colors are made or read aloud informative picture books. Also select some picture books that exhibit different media (tissue paper, clay, collage, watercolor) and interesting use of color. The following books are excellent selections as books to share:

- Hoban, Tana. *Colors Everywhere.* Greenwillow, 1994.
- Jonas, Ann. *Color Dance.* Greenwillow, 1989.
- Koningsburg, E. L. *Samuel Todd's Book of Great Colors.* Atheneum, 1990.

· · · · · The Dramatic Play Center · · · · ·

Transform this center into a "Color Shop" or art and craft supply store. Gather a variety of colorful scraps (tissue paper squares, gift wrap, ribbon, construction paper, cellophane) for the children to "purchase" at the store. Be sure to include other plastic items that are colorful, play money, cash register, chart paper, telephone, play clay (various colors), colored pencils, paper, and other kinds of art supplies that children can use. *Note:* If it is possible, try to contact local artists for the children to visit or invite the artists to your classroom. These experiences are wonderful opportunities for children to gain insight into how professional people work with color as well as providing rich ideas for their play.

ACTIVITIES FOR CURRICULUM AREAS

READING & LANGUAGE DEVELOPMENT CENTER ACTIVITIES

· · · · · Looking for Colors · · · · ·

Materials Needed: picture card patterns on page 203, scissors, construction paper, glue, markers, cassette tape, tape recorder and player

Directions: Look around for colors that are mentioned in this delightful rhyme. Perhaps you might wish to share the following rhyme during group time. Talk about the rhyming words that are heard at the ends of the lines. To prepare the center materials, reproduce the pattern page and mount it on the construction paper. Cut apart the cards and color them as desired. Provide a recording of the rhyme. In the center, have the child listen to the rhyme and then arrange the pictures in sequential order. When finished, ask the child to tell you which words at the end of the lines rhyme. Another suggestion: Print the poem on chart paper. Attach Velcro buttons at the end of each line and on the back of the picture cards. Have the children arrange the pictures in the corresponding places while listening to the poem.

Colors

Red, red. I see red.
    It's an apple growing overhead.
Yellow, yellow. I see yellow.
    A big banana, long and mellow.
Orange, orange. Can it be?
    An orange growing on a tree.
Blue, blue. I see blue.
    My kitten's eyes–she says, "Mew, mew."

Green, green. I see green.
    From my garden, one string bean.
Purple, purple. What do I see?
    Grapes on a vine, just for me!
White, white. I see white.
    Fluffy clouds, so soft and light.
              –Unknown

· · · · · A Colorful Alphabet Game · · · · ·

Materials Needed: game board patterns on pages 204–206, poster board, markers, glue, milk jug caps or poster board circles, permanent marker

Directions: With this game children can practice matching lowercase letters with capitals. Just collect 26 milk jug caps (cut out poster board circles) and print the capital letters on the manipulative with a permanent marker. Reproduce the game board patterns by enlarging the images before duplicating them on large copier paper. Mount the game board on poster board by gluing the sections together and then color the pictures as desired. Be sure to color the balloons with the corresponding colors. For the activity have the child match the capital letter with the lowercase letter by placing it on the board.

· · · · · Color Cats with Hats · · · · ·

Materials Needed: picture card patterns on page 207, construction paper, scissors, glue

Directions: Look at these color cats that wear such interesting hats. Young learners only need to think about each cat's color and match them with the correct words. To prepare the materials, make a copy of the picture cards and mount them on construction paper. If you prefer to have the children match color with word, cover the color word beneath each cat before making the photocopy of the pattern page. Cut apart the picture cards and color them. Print the color words on separate cards. Set aside the Calico Cat for a color game. In the center encourage the child to match colors and words. Some children may prefer to play a matching game with the colored cats. Provide two copies of each picture card and adapt the game rules for Old Maid, except the wild card is the Calico Cat.

· · · · · Where Is Bug? · · · · ·

Materials Needed: picture card patterns on page 208, construction paper, scissors, glue

Directions: Look carefully at the pictures so you can answer the question "Where is Bug?" To prepare the cards reproduce them at 100% or enlarge them to fit on 11" x 17" (279 x 432 mm) paper. Mount the copy on construction paper and cut apart the picture cards. Have the child look at the pictures and tell a partner where bug is in relation to the crayon. Some children may be ready to identify pairs of cards that have opposite meanings, such as on and off, above and below. If appropriate, the materials also can be used for a matching activity by providing a second copy of the picture cards. The child can match identical pictures.

· · · · · A Little Mouse in a Color House · · · · ·

Materials Needed: patterns on page 209, small milk cartons, markers, scissors, glue, construction paper

Directions: Where is the little mouse? For this activity the children must guess in which color house the mouse is hiding. To prepare the materials, copy the pattern to make the following houses: orange, blue, red, green, yellow, pink, and purple. Mount the copies on construction paper for durability and color each house with light and dark shades. Duplicate the mouse and color it as desired. Cut out the houses and mouse. To prepare the milk cartons, cut off the tops so the milk cartons will stand upside down. Glue each house to a milk carton. In the center, have the child work with a partner. One player hides the mouse under a house and the other player must state the following rhyme to guess where the mouse is. For example: "Little mouse, little mouse, are you in the *yellow* house?" The player checks under the yellow house. Repeat until the mouse is found. Let the children take turns hiding the mouse and searching for it.

white cat

black cat

gray cat

orange cat

brown cat

calico cat

in

out

on

off

above

below

behind

in front

red

yellow

blue

WRITING CENTER ACTIVITIES

· · · · · Lots of Colorful Things · · · · ·

Materials Needed: magazines, crayons, markers, stapler, paper, tissue paper, scraps of construction paper, pencils, paste

Directions: Here is an opportunity for the child to make a color book. So many different things can be featured in this book. For example: Red is an apple, cherry, rose, and a ripe strawberry. Green is grass, string beans, peas, and the branches of an evergreen tree. Orange is an orange, pumpkin, carrot, and the beak of a parrot. To prepare the materials print sentence strips for the child to use. For example: Red is _____. *Note:* Be sure to print the color word with dashed lines on each sentence strip. Make enough copies for each child. To make a color booklet for each child, bind several sheets of paper, one page for each color. Have the child cut apart the sentence strips and glue each one on a page. Let the child trace over the color word and finish the sentence with a picture or word of something that displays the color. Some children will include pictures of other things in the same color. Have the child continue until a page is completed for each color.

Variation: What is in each color house? Of course, only items that match the house. For this activity, reproduce the color house patterns on page 209, one for each color. Display the houses on a poster board and color each one as desired. Let the children find pictures of objects that have the identical colors. Glue the item near the house and label it. Now you have a large chart for the child to use when working on her color book.

· · · · · Card Shop · · · · ·

Materials Needed: glue sticks or paste, construction paper, markers, colored pencils, tissue paper, scissors, craft items, paper scraps, crayons

Directions: Children can make "greeting cards" to give to family members/guardians by decorating construction paper and then printing a special colorful message in each card. Place the gathered materials on a tray or small table in the center. Provide some models for the children to view by folding the paper in different forms. Be sure to include samples of commercial and computer-generated cards.

· · · · · Stringing Colorful Cereal · · · · ·

Materials Needed: fruit-flavored "O"-shaped cereal, yarn, masking tape, plastic container, tray

Directions: The children can certainly thread cereal on yarn and enjoy a snack later. For this fine motor activity, cut a length of yarn for each child. Tie a large knot at one end and wrap a piece of masking tape on the other end. In the center, encourage the child to thread 20 pieces of cereal on the string. If you would like the child to work with a pattern, start the pattern on the string for him. Pour some of the cereal on a tray so the child can easily pick up pieces without touching others. When finished, tie the string into a loop and let the child wear his colorful snack.

· · · · · Berry Colors · · · · ·

Materials Needed: pattern on page 209, tissue paper, glue, pencil, pictures of berries on plants, scissors, construction paper

Directions: Berries are found in abundance in nature—blueberries, blackberries, strawberries, as well as poisonous berries. To prepare the materials, make three or more copies of the berry baskets and glue them on 3" x 6" (76 x 152 mm) construction paper strips. Print each color word on a strip—such as red, blue and orange. Glue a few tissue paper "berries" in each corresponding basket. Prepare additional paper strips for each child by cutting paper strips on the paper cutter and then gluing a basket on each one. In the center let the child glue "berries" in a basket and print the corresponding color word on the strip. To make a berry, take one piece of tissue paper and roll it into a ball. Glue the berry in the basket. Continue making berries until the basket is full. Repeat the process for the other color strips.

· · · · · Printing in Finger Paints · · · · ·

Materials Needed: finger paint paper, finger paints (red, yellow, pink, blue, green), spoon, paper towels, smock

Directions: Just decide which colors to use and then have the children cover the paper with wonderful colors. When finished, let them print the color words within the corresponding splashes of colors.

MATH CENTER ACTIVITIES

· · · · · Colorful Shapes · · · · ·

Materials Needed: patterns on page 214, attribute blocks, markers, scissors, construction paper or poster board

Directions: So much to do if you sort by shape or color. To prepare the materials, make four copies of the pattern page, each one in a different color (red, yellow, blue, green). Mount the copies on construction paper or poster board. Cut out the shapes. (*Optional:* You may wish to laminate the pieces for durability.) In the center, encourage the child to work with a partner. The children can sort the shapes by color, size or shape. If you have attribute blocks, let the child sort the blocks with the cutouts.

Variation: Provide large templates of the following shapes: triangle, square, rectangle, circle, hexagon and diamond. Let the child trace around each shape on construction paper and glue yarn on the outlines. When the project is completed, it is a "Shape Collage." The child may enjoy finding pictures of objects in these shapes. Just add those pictures to the collage.

· · · · · Counting Crayons · · · · ·

Materials Needed: picture card patterns on pages 215–216, plastic or foam numerals, markers, scissors, construction paper, box of 64 old crayons

Directions: How many crayons are in the stack? Children will count and then match the sets with the correct numerals. To prepare the materials, reproduce the pattern pages and mount them on construction paper. Color the copies as desired and cut apart the cards. In the center, ask the child to count the crayons on each card and then place the correct numeral near the card. When finished, encourage the child to ask a partner to check her work.

Variation: Matching sets of crayons can be made by counting old crayons and placing the corresponding set with each picture card.

····· Colorful Number Parade ·····

Materials Needed: pattern on page 216, construction paper, markers, scissors, glue

Directions: Here is a colorful line of cars that challenges young mathematicians. The cars must be arranged in numerical order. To prepare the materials, make seven copies of the pattern page and mount them on construction paper. Color the cars as desired and print a numeral on each one using a black marker. (*Optional:* You may wish to laminate the cars for durability.) In the center, let the children arrange the cars accordingly.

Variation: Some children may benefit from counting sets of math manipulatives that correspond with the cars.

····· Measuring with Crayons ·····

Materials Needed: pattern on page 209, bulletin board paper, markers, tempera paints, scissors, glue, box of new crayons

Directions: Using crayons for "colorful" tools the young learner can measure anything in the classroom, even giant-size crayons. Using the opaque project, enlarge the crayon pattern to a preferred size on bulletin board paper. (You may wish to make the crayons about the same height as the children.) Make more than one crayon shape for decorating the room. Finish the decorations by painting them with tempera paints. In the center, provide one giant crayon and a set of new crayons. Let the children measure the giant cutout with the crayons. They may also be interested in comparing their heights with the crayon.

····· Let's Count Buttons and Beans ·····

Materials Needed: bright colored buttons, lima beans, paint, index cards, markers

Directions: With cards that show numerals, your young learners can make delightful sets of buttons and beans. With very little preparation, the activity materials can be ready. Paint lima beans in bright colors and allow them to dry. Print numerals on index cards in various marker colors. Place the beans, buttons and cards on a tray in the center. Let the child make the corresponding sets for the number cards.

Variation: Try making button and bean patterns. Reproduce the pattern mat on page 193. Begin some patterns for the children to finish: AAB, ABB, or ABAB.

Counting Crayons Picture Card Patterns

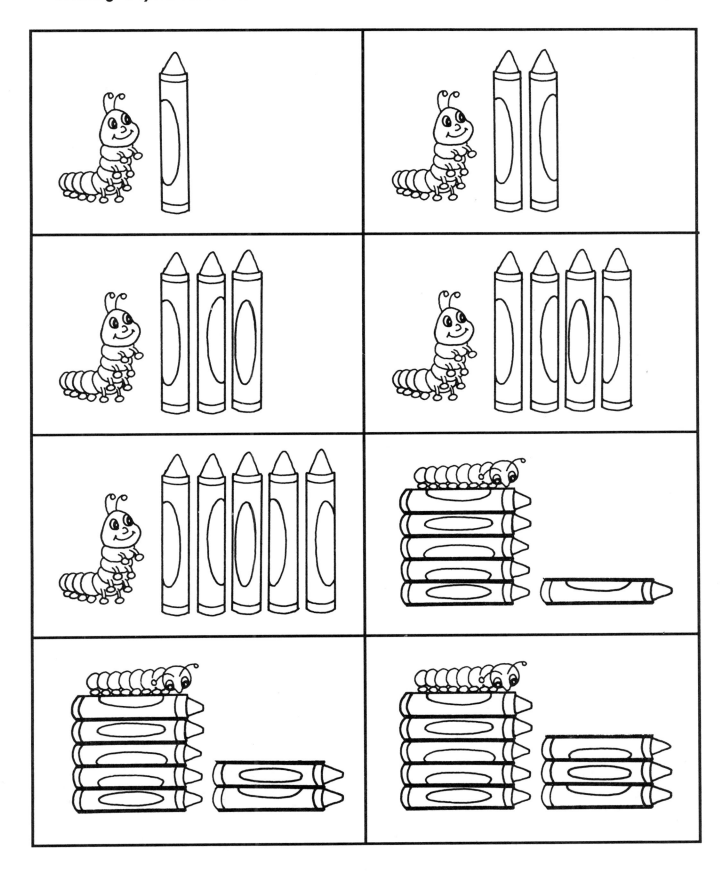

Counting Crayons Picture Card Patterns/
Colorful Number Parade Patterns

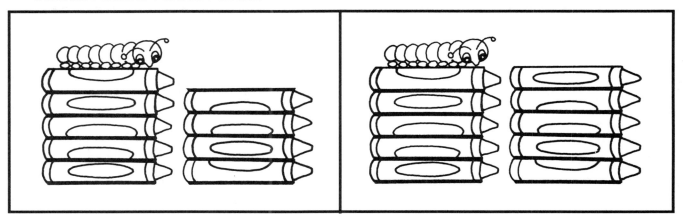

SCIENCE CENTER ACTIVITIES

· · · · · A Rainbow on the Wall · · · · ·

Materials Needed: small pan, mirror, water, paper, colored pencils

Directions: Yes, it is possible to see a rainbow on the classroom wall. To do this, just pick a sunny spot on the classroom floor. Place a mirror in a small pan of water and set the equipment in the sunbeam. Keep part of the mirror in the water as you try holding the mirror at different angles. *Note:* The light travels through the water and then is reflected off the mirror (portion in the water). The reflection from the mirror can be seen on the wall. If you have the right angle, you will see a rainbow of colors or a spectrum. Let the children experiment with the mirror and water. When they have produced a spectrum have them draw pictures and "write" about what they learned.

Variation: Locate a prism that the children can use during this investigation about spectrums.

· · · · · Sorting by Colors · · · · ·

Materials Needed: various objects for sorting (eight basic colors), file folders or poster board, scissors, glue

Directions: For this sorting activity, ask parents and caregivers to lend items from home. Ask the children to bring objects having bright solid colors (picnic dishes and flatware, buttons, small toys). Also search the classroom for items (math manipulatives, markers, pencils, scissors with colored handles, erasers) to add the collection. To prepare the materials, make a label for each color. Glue the labels on the file folders or pieces of poster board to make sorting mats. Color the labels, if appropriate, to help the children identify the color words. Set all of the materials in a large container. In the center, have the children sort the objects by color and place them on the sorting mats.

· · · · · Swirls of Colors · · · · ·

Materials Needed: food coloring (red, yellow, blue), cold water, small plastic cups, flat toothpicks, smocks, Styrofoam trays, plastic pail

Directions: This delightful activity will engage young scientists in color investigations. It may be a little messy so keep an old towel handy for cleanup. To set up the center, provide cold water in a large container and a plastic pail for cleanup. The rest of the work will be done by the children. Let the child partially fill a plastic cup and choose two colors of food coloring. Carefully add one drop of each color to the water. Watch how the colors eventually mix or use the toothpick to mix them. When the child is finished observing the results, empty the cup into the pail. Repeat the process with other colors of food coloring.

· · · · · Colorful Finger Paints · · · · ·

Materials Needed: flour, salt, measuring cups, mustard for yellow color, powdered fruit drinks (natural dye for green, blue and red), food coloring, finger paint paper, large spoon

Directions: Making the finger paints is part of the process for this science activity. This time children will have an opportunity to prepare the special paints. Create an instruction card for the children to follow:
> 1 cup (237 ml) flour
> ¼ cup (59 ml) salt
> colored water
> Mix together. Add enough water for paint consistency.

In the center have the children follow the instruction card to make the paint, coloring it with a natural dye (foods) or food coloring. When finished, let them paint pictures.

· · · · · Color Paddles · · · · ·

Materials Needed: acetate from folder covers (red, blue, yellow), poster board, flashlight, scissors, glue, utility knife

Directions: What fun it is to look at things through these color paddles! To make the paddles, cut out six identical paddle shapes from poster board. Using a utility knife, cut out the center of each paddle. Place a sheet of colored acetate between two paddles and glue them together to hold the acetate in place. Repeat the process for other colors. Now the paddles are ready for young scientists to investigate color.

ART CENTER ACTIVITIES

· · · · · Clay Creations · · · · ·

Materials Needed: play clay (red, blue, pink, yellow, brown, green, purple, white, orange), craft sticks, art tray, cookie-cutter shapes, plastic knives

Directions: Sculptures, patterns, shapes, all are possible when working with clay. Mold the clay into animals, people, vehicles, and more. Cut out shapes and arrange them in a pattern. Decorate shapes with other colors of clay. Roll the clay and make coils. Use the coils to build vase. There are endless possibilities for the children to create by using the gathered materials in the art center.

· · · · · Watercolor Surprises · · · · ·

Materials Needed: watercolor paints, paintbrush, paper, white crayon, water, smock

Directions: To make a surprise picture, have the child draw a picture (zigzag lines, swirls, objects, scene) using a white crayon and then cover the paper with watercolors. The crayon drawing will appear through the paint. This is known as a crayon resist.

· · · · · 3-D Paper Sculptures · · · · ·

Materials Needed: small poster board sheets, construction paper strips (various widths, lengths and colors), glue, paper cutter, scissors

Directions: It is fun to create paper sculptures that look like bridges, steps, roadways, roller coasters and more. Let the children work with partners for this cooperative building project. Cut construction paper into strips of various widths and lengths and then show the children how to glue the end of the strip on the poster board by folding and gluing a tab. The possibilities are endless as the dimensional masterpieces take form.

· · · · · Colorful Magic · · · · ·

Materials Needed: finger paint paper, tempera paints (primary colors), spoons, waxed paper

Directions: Here is an opportunity for young fingers to work magic by blending paint colors to make other colors. To do this, sprinkle tempera paints on the finger paint paper. *Note:* Be sure some drops are placed closely together so the child can make green, purple and orange by blending the paints. Cover the paper with a large piece of waxed paper. Let the child spread the paint by rubbing the waxed paper. When finished, allow the paint to dry before removing the waxed paper. *Optional:* The painted creations can be cut into shapes of butterflies or kites that have tissue paper tails. You may wish to hang them in your classroom for a dynamic display of color!

· · · · · Textured Collages · · · · ·

Materials Needed: scraps of fabric (bright colors, interesting bold patterns), tissue paper (assorted colors), glue, paper, scissors, assorted craft materials, colorful buttons, felt pieces

Directions: Gather various items for creating colorful textured collages. Encourage the child to select colors and textures and glue the items on the paper.

TOOTHY GRINS

Learning about our teeth and how to take care of them are important issues for young children. Helping children learn to accept the responsibility of taking care of their teeth begins at a young age. During this unit of study, the children will examine their teeth, find out how they use their teeth to cut (incisors), tear (canine) or grind (molars) food, talk about oral hygiene and healthy foods to eat, and discover how their teeth are similar to animals' teeth.

To prepare for this theme, you may wish to change your classroom into an environment about dental health by using the patterns on page 232. Using the opaque projector, trace the patterns on large sheets of paper. Paint them before displaying them on the walls.

As you set up your centers, be sure to include books about teeth, oral hygiene and animals' teeth for the children to read in your library corner. During group time talk about dental health or read aloud informative picture books. The following books have useful information or are wonderful for sharing:
- DeSantis, Kenny. *A Dentist's Tools.* Dodd, Mead & Company, 1988.
- Falwell, Cathryn. *Dragon Tooth.* Clarion Books, 1996
- Pluckrose, Henry. *Look at Teeth.* Franklin Watts, 1988.
- Rogers, Fred. *Going to the Dentist.* G.P. Putnam's Sons. 1989.

· · · · · The Dramatic Play Center · · · · ·

Transform this area into a dental office. If possible, display posters about teeth and dental hygiene. Also provide a telephone, pencils, papers, latex gloves, plastic glasses, masks, dental bib, toothbrushes, dental floss, unbreakable mirror, small table, chairs, magazines, chart paper, markers, dolls, play tools for dental work, appointment cards, play money, models of teeth, and more. Perhaps a local dental office will donate a bib and gloves for the children to use. As you set up the dental office, try to arrange the props so there are several mini-areas: waiting room, an appointment area and a dental examination room. Now the center is ready for the children to choose their roles and socially interact being the dentist, assistant, patient, and so on.

ACTIVITIES FOR CURRICULUM AREAS

READING & LANGUAGE DEVELOPMENT CENTER ACTIVITIES

· · · · · Caring for Your Teeth Story · · · · ·

Materials Needed: picture card patterns on page 225, construction paper, scissors, glue, markers

Directions: When do you brush your teeth? What foods should you eat for healthy teeth? For this activity children can share with partners how they care for their teeth. To set up the center, reproduce the pattern page and mount it on construction paper. Cut apart the cards and color them if desired. Invite the child to study the cards carefully and tell her partner a story about how she cares for her teeth.

Variation: Set the stage for "big" stories. Enlarge the pictures on 11" x 17" (279 x 432 mm) copier paper and display them in the language arts center.

· · · · · Big "T" Puzzle · · · · ·

Materials Needed: poster board, scissors, glue, markers, magazines, patterns on page 232

Directions: Here is a giant puzzle that needs to be solved. To prepare the puzzle for the center, draw a large bold outline of the letter "T." Make a photocopy of the shape patterns, cut them out and glue them on the letter. Color the pictures as desired. Cut out the letter and then cut it apart into puzzle pieces. Be sure to have a different picture on each puzzle piece. If it is possible, clip pictures from magazines that show people smiling. Also glue these pictures on the puzzle pieces. Now this "Big T" puzzle is ready for the children to assemble.

Variation: A "Little T" puzzle can also be made for the children to assemble in the center. Just draw the lowercase "t" on poster board and cut it apart in puzzle pieces. Glue pictures on the pieces to complete the puzzle.

····· I Can Rhyme Puzzles ·····

Materials Needed: patterns on pages 226–227, construction paper, scissors, glue, markers

Directions: Sort, assemble pieces and rhyme! What a delightful way to think about pictures/words while assembling small puzzles. To prepare the two miniature puzzles, enlarge and photocopy the pattern pages and then mount them on construction paper. Color the pictures with markers. Because it is difficult for some children to assemble puzzles, use a marker to give each puzzle a different colored frame. Finish the set of puzzles by cutting apart the pictures on the dashed lines. In the center, the children may assemble the puzzles and talk about the pictures. When the rhyming words are identified, have the child explain the pairs of rhyming words to a partner.

····· My Teeth Lotto ·····

Materials Needed: lotto board pattern on page 228, construction paper, scissors, glue, markers

Directions: What are the parts of a tooth? What do we use to take care of our teeth? These picture cards are useful in conveying information about dental health. This visual discrimination activity can easily be adapted to meet the needs of your young learners. Decide if the children will either match pictures or words. To prepare the materials, reproduce the pattern page two times. If a lotto board must show words without pictures (refer to pattern page 16), cover the pictures on the pattern page before making the second photocopy. Mount the copies on construction paper. Cut apart one set of the picture cards to make the playing cards. In the center, invite the child to match the picture cards with pictures or words on the playing board.

····· Opposites ·····

Materials Needed: picture cards pattern on page 229, construction paper, scissors, glue, markers

Directions: What is the opposite of on? hot? smile? outside? These questions can be answered by the children as they work with the picture cards. To prepare the materials, photocopy the pattern page and mount it on construction paper. Cut apart the picture cards and color them if desired. In the center have the child find the pairs of pictures which demonstrate the concept of opposites.

brush teeth

brush teeth

brush tongue

floss teeth

eat healthy foods

checked by dentist

dog

log

fever

beaver

 # My Teeth Lotto

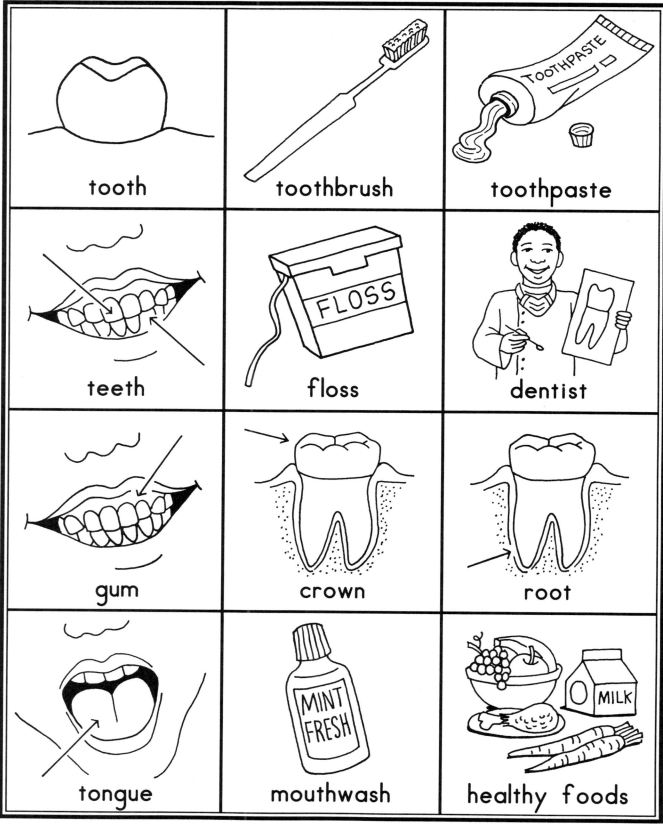

tooth	toothbrush	toothpaste
teeth	floss	dentist
gum	crown	root
tongue	mouthwash	healthy foods

inside

outside

on

off

hot

cold

smile

frown

WRITING CENTER

• • • • • Teeth Notes • • • • •

Materials Needed: pattern on page 232, paper, pencils, toy telephone

Directions: Using the tooth pattern create tooth-shaped notepads for the children to use. To do this, enlarge the pattern of a molar and make several copies for each child. In the center, let the child "pretend" to use the telephone and take messages about teeth and dental care. The child can draw, write or scribble notes on the paper. Provide a place for her to hang her notes when she is finished writing them.

• • • • • All About Teeth Booklet • • • • •

Materials Needed: booklet cover pattern on page 233, paper, pencils, scissors, markers, colored pencils, stapler, paste

Directions: Here is an idea for making booklets to help children share what they have learned about teeth and dental health. The child can choose what to feature on the booklet cover or use the booklet cover pattern. Assemble a few sheets of newsprint for the booklet pages and cover with construction paper. Staple or tie the pages together with yarn. Provide reproduced copies of the pattern pages for the child to use when writing about teeth. Some children may wish to use the small pictures on the lotto board pattern (page 228) to write rebus stories.

Variation: Decorate the learning center with pictures and words. Just enlarge the small lotto board pictures (page 228) and display them on poster board. If appropriate, the young writers can copy the words on tooth-shape word cards.

· · · · · Toothbrush Strokes · · · · ·

Materials Needed: finger paint paper, finger paint, smock, old toothbrushes

Directions: With a couple dabs of finger paint the child can create interesting zigzag lines and small circular continuous lines (same motion for brushing along the gum line) by painting with a toothbrush on paper. Encourage the child to also use an up and down motion when painting lines. Of course, have the child finish by printing the letter "Tt" in the paint.

· · · · · Brushing My Teeth Chart · · · · ·

Materials Needed: construction paper, markers, pencils, two colors of foil stars

Directions: Encourage the child to draw a picture of himself and write about how he will care for his teeth. Ask the child if he brushed his teeth today. If he did care for his teeth, have him place a star on his paper. Let the child bring the chart and five to seven stars of each color to his house. Encourage him to add a star to the chart each time he brushes his teeth and a different colored star when he flosses his teeth.

Variation: It is always helpful to include a note to parents/caregivers about this project so they can encourage the child to complete the chart.

· · · · · Printing Special Words · · · · ·

Materials Needed: patterns on page 232, scissors, pencils

Directions: Enlarge the toothbrush, toothpaste, floss container, and molar on large copier paper for special word cards. Print the name of each object on the shape. Make additional copies of the shapes for each child. Cut apart the shapes and place them in a labeled container. Display the prepared word cards in the center. Invite the child to select a shape and print its name on the word card. When finished, display the word card in the center.

Variation: For giant-size wall decorations, use the opaque projector to enlarge the pattern shapes on bulletin board paper and then trace them. When finished print the names of the objects on the shapes. Color them as desired and display them in the center.

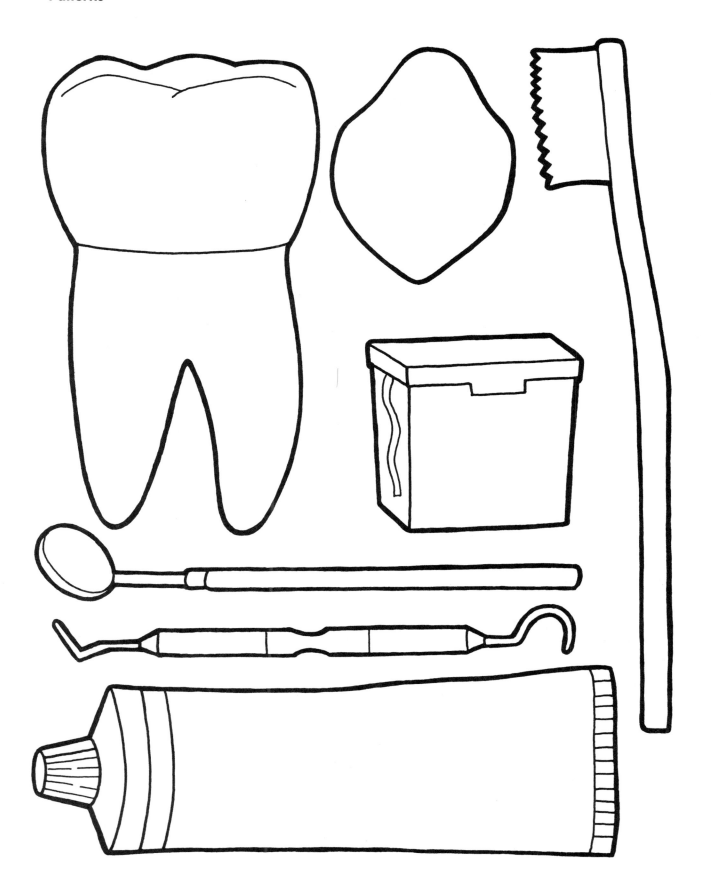

All About Teeth

MATH CENTER ACTIVITIES

· · · · · Tooth Count · · · · ·

Materials Needed: molar pattern on page 232, paper, marker, scissors, mirror

Directions: During this unit of study your young learners will discover that they have 20 teeth in their mouths. Upon closer examination they will observe that not all of their teeth look like the molar pattern. However, to reinforce that each child has 20 baby teeth or primary teeth, have the children arrange the cutouts in numerical order. To prepare the materials, enlarge the molar pattern and make 20 teeth. Mount them on construction paper. Number each one 1 to 20 and then cut out the teeth. In the center have the child count to 20 and arrange the teeth in the correct sequence.

· · · · · Counting Sets of Toothbrushes · · · · ·

Materials Needed: six empty frozen juice cans, toothbrushes, markers, decorative self-adhesive paper

Directions: For this counting and comparing activity collect empty juice cans (six cans) and decorate them with self-adhesive paper to make toothbrush holders. Number the cans 3 to 8. Collect approximately 30 toothbrushes for this activity. Parents/caregivers may be willing to donate toothbrushes. (If the brushes need to be sanitized, soak them in a weak bleach solution and then rinse with water.) In the center, let the child work with a partner. One child selects three cans randomly and fills each one with the corresponding number of brushes. When finished, the partner checks the work and then places one additional brush next to each set. The first player must tell how large each new set is. Repeat the process so the partner has a turn.

Variations: One child may also remove one brush from each set of brushes and then ask the partner to tell how many brushes are in each set. A book for reinforcing the skill of comparing numbers is *One More and One Less* by Giulio Maestro (Crown Publishers, Inc., 1974). Let the children read this book before making sets that differ by one item.

· · · · · Patterning with Toothbrushes · · · · ·

Materials Needed: pattern on page 232 or actual toothbrushes, construction paper, scissors, markers, glue

Directions: For this repeat patterning activity, either collect several toothbrushes in three different colors or make copies of the toothbrush pattern and color them as desired. Mount the copies on construction paper and then cut out the shapes. If you prefer, use the toothbrush cutouts to make patterns on construction paper. Glue the pieces in place and provide additional cutouts or toothbrushes for the child to use in continuing the pattern. In the center, show the child a pattern to continue with the cutouts or toothbrushes. Repeat the process with other patterns.

· · · · · Measuring with Toothbrushes · · · · ·

Materials Needed: 15–20 toothbrushes (with identical length)

Directions: How far is it across the classroom? How many toothbrush lengths is the teacher's desk? Many large items in the classroom can be measured with toothbrushes. Be imaginative and encourage the children to investigate lengths. Be sure to encourage them to compare their results. What is 2 toothbrushes longer in length than a book? a shoe?

Variation: One interesting feature about the canine tooth is how it varies in size in different animals' mouths, such as the tiger or jaguar and the tyrannosaurus. One idea for a measurement activity is to enlarge the canine pattern on page 232 according to the size of an actual tooth in the tiger's mouth, a dog's and the tyrannosaurus's. Supply math manipulatives for the children to use when measuring these cutouts.

· · · · · Comparing Weights · · · · ·

Materials Needed: several tubes of toothpaste (varying in weight and size), bucket balance, math counters

Directions: Which tube weighs the most? the least? For this activity, obtain several tubes of toothpaste and a bucket balance. (Be sure to provide at least two identical-looking tubes that do not weigh the same because some toothpaste has been removed from one of the tubes.) In the center, encourage the child to investigate which tube weighs the most or the least. If the child is working with three or four tubes, have him arrange them in order according to weight when finished.

SCIENCE CENTER ACTIVITIES

· · · · · Looking at Toothpaste · · · · ·

Materials Needed: three different kinds of toothpaste, magnifying glass, waxed paper

Directions: How are toothpastes alike? different? What do they feel like? These are some questions the children can investigate. In the center, encourage the child to examine a small dab of each toothpaste. (Be sure the cap is secure on each tube.) Let the child use the magnifying glass to observe the toothpaste. Next have her smell and taste each paste. Encourage her to work with a partner to talk about their conclusions regarding the flavor, texture and smell of each toothpaste. When they are finished making their observations, ask them to specify which toothpastes they prefer. This is a perfect opportunity to graph the results.

Variation: How does toothpaste clean a surface? To find out, allow pancake syrup to air dry on a Styrofoam plate and then clean the plate by brushing toothpaste on it with a wet brush.

· · · · · Toothy Grins · · · · ·

Materials Needed: picture card patterns on page 238, scissors, construction paper, glue, unbreakable mirror, nature magazines

Directions: Look closely at the teeth in your mouth. How are they similar? different? Why is the shape of the tooth important? Can you identify the incisors, the canines and the molars? Children can think about these questions as they study their teeth. To prepare the materials, photocopy the pattern page and mount it on construction paper. Cut apart the cards. In the center, place the picture cards along with a mirror in a labeled container. Invite the child to look in a mirror and describe to a partner what he sees. When the children are finished observing their teeth, have them study the picture cards and decide which teeth are like the animals' teeth. For example, the incisors in the person's mouth are similar to the front teeth in the beaver's mouth. When the child is finished comparing teeth, encourage him to locate other pictures of animals' teeth and compare them with his own.

· · · · · Decay Observation · · · · ·

Materials Needed: apples, marshmallow fluff, plastic knives, paper towels, lemon juice, pastry brush

Directions: During group time discuss what happens to a tooth when it starts to decay. In the center, prepare some apples by cutting them into quarters or eighths. Cover about half of the cut surface of each apple with lemon juice. It is important to not treat some of the surface because it must turn brown. Later, the child needs to fix the "decay" in the apple by removing it like a dentist. Instead of using a drill have the child use a plastic knife to cut out the brown surface and then fill the space with the marshmallow fluff like a filling in a tooth. (*Note:* the marshmallow fluff is easy to spread and makes the surface white again.)

· · · · · Caring for Our Teeth · · · · ·

Materials Needed: small paper cups, large unbreakable mirror, cotton swabs, scissors, water, magazines, glue, paper

Directions: Here is an activity to help the children practice taking care of their teeth. During group time discuss how certain foods (like apples) actually clean the teeth while others (sweet gummy foods) stick to the surface of a tooth. In the center, let the child practice "brushing" his front teeth with a cotton swab by moving it in small circles on the teeth. This can be done while looking in a mirror and showing this procedure to a partner. The children may also clip pictures from magazines of healthy food choices. Have them glue the pictures on the paper along with pictures of people smiling.

· · · · · Inventing a "Mouthwash" · · · · ·

Materials Needed: small paper cups, water, plastic droppers, smock, peppermint extract, plastic cup, measuring cup, small plastic bottles, poster board, food coloring, marker

Directions: For this activity, just provide a recipe and the necessary items so the young scientist can prepare this "mouthwash." On a small poster board, copy the following recipe and include simple drawings of the items: ¼ cup (.12 ml) water, 1 drop peppermint extract, and 1 drop food coloring. Mix in a cup and pour into a bottle. In the center let the child follow the instructions and mix "mouthwash." *Note:* Be sure she does not taste the solution. When the solution is made, let the child pour it into a bottle and label it.

incisors

canines

molars

ART CENTER ACTIVITIES

· · · · · Floss Art · · · · ·

Materials Needed: dental floss, tempera paints, construction paper

Directions: Perhaps you are familiar with string painting to make swirls and streaks of color on paper. Well, instead of using string provide wide dental floss for the children to pull through the paint. To make the design, let the child fold a piece of construction paper in half. Scatter two or three dabs of paint onto one side of the paper. Give the child a long piece of dental floss and have her loop the string through the paint, leaving one end of the string beyond the edge of the paper. Encourage the child to close the paper in half like a book and pull the string out of the folded paper. When finished open the paper to see the design. If interested, encourage the child to repeat the process by adding drops of a second color of paint to the design and pulling the string through them. Of course, some children will be interested in making several string designs.

Variation: Perhaps two different colors of tempera paint can be used at the same time to make colorful designs.

· · · · · Toothbrush Painting · · · · ·

Materials Needed: old window screen, paper, smock, tempera paint, toothbrushes, newspaper, smock

Directions: Splatter painting and toothbrush creations! Just another way to recycle old toothbrushes in the classroom. To prepare the materials for this center activity, obtain a square piece of window screen and wrap the edges in duct tape or have a carpenter set the screen in a wooden frame. *Note:* This is important because the edges are sharp. Place the frame with paper, old toothbrushes and paint in a labeled tub. In the center, encourage the child to create splatter paintings by holding the screen above his paper and rubbing the paint-covered toothbrush across the screen. Be sure the area is covered with newspaper to ensure that cleanup is easier. The child may also paint a picture on the paper by using a toothbrush instead of a paintbrush. Hopefully, the child is wearing a smock during these projects because splatter painting is messy work.

· · · · · Shaving Cream Teeth · · · · ·

Materials Needed: shaving cream, craft sticks, Styrofoam trays, plastic mirror

Directions: For these shaving cream creations let the child get started by squeezing a small amount of shaving cream (about the size of a cupcake) on a tray. Encourage her to sculpt a tooth or teeth out of the shaving cream. It make be helpful for the child to look at her teeth in a mirror, especially if she is adding indentations and ridges to her sculpture. Some children may prefer to use the shaving cream as finger paint and then paint pictures of pearly white teeth.

· · · · · Dental Models · · · · ·

Materials Needed: project clay (recipe on page 30), craft sticks, dental floss, plastic teeth models (available at party supply stores), toothbrushes, wide dental floss

Directions: Teeth, dental tools and toothbrushes are just a few of the items that can be created in clay. To prepare the materials, follow the recipe for making the project clay. In the center let the child work with the clay to make dental related items. Be sure to demonstrate how you can cut the clay into small pieces with the dental floss. This may be helpful when the child is shaping a tooth or a set of teeth out of clay.

· · · · · My Teeth Poster · · · · ·

Materials Needed: magazines, markers, paper, ruler, crayons, paste, small old toothbrushes, dental floss, toothpaste cartons, white glitter (diamond dust), glue stick

Directions: Here is an idea for combining children's interest in using glitter with dental health. To do this, let the children clip pictures of people smiling from magazines. Of course, encourage them to find other pictures that relate to their care of teeth. Have the children paste the pictures on the construction paper to make posters. They also may glue on pieces of dental floss, portions of toothpaste cartons and so on. When they are pleased with their arrangements, encourage them to give the "smiles" a pearly white sparkle by gluing white glitter on the teeth in some pictures. Wow!